My Daughter a Preacher!?!

★ ★ ★

Leslie B. Flynn

★ ★ ★

My Daughter a Preacher!?!

My Daughter a Preacher!?!

Copyright © 1996, Leslie B. Flynn

All Scripture quotations, unless otherwise specified, are taken from *The King James Version* of the Bible.

Scriptures marked NIV are from the *New International Version* of the Bible (Copyright © 1973, 1978, 1984 International Bible Society. Used by permission of Zondervan Bible Publishers. All rights reserved.)

ISBN: 1-896400-10-8

To order more copies contact:
Leslie B. Flynn, 32 Highview Ave.,
Nanuet, NY 10954 USA
(914) 623-3319

Printed in Canada

To my seven daughters

*whose sweet dispositions
and
initiative, ingenuity and industry
have long been a source of delight
to their mother and me*

Linnea	*(psychodramatist and professor of nursing)*
Janna	*(minister)*
Marilee	*(artist)*
Annilee	*(lawyer)*
Donna	*(database analyst)*
Carol	*(teacher)*
Susan	*(telecommunications engineer)*

Table of Contents

★ ★ ★

Preface

★ ★ ★

My daughter — a minister, a preacher??

My daughter — a reverend, a pastor!!

I recall the surprise the day I, a pastor, learned of my daughter's decision to enter the ministry. In her late thirties, happily married and successful in business, she felt an irresistible call to enroll in seminary.

At first, the news brought me great delight. Since I have seven daughters, but no son, I could never have a son in the ministry. Now I would have a daughter following in the same calling.

However, on second thought, my emotions were mixed. I had been raised in an atmosphere which disapproved of women preachers. For forty years I had pastored in a denomination which, though giving women much latitude in church ministries, had more than once passed resolutions affirming that the office of pastor-teacher should remain the God-given responsibility of men.

Naturally, with all the media and ecclesiastical attention focused on the role of women in the church, I had been doing some thinking on the subject. Now I would have to do more.

This book is the story of a pastor-father's contemplation on his daughter's decision to enter the ministry. With no pretense of complete, in-depth coverage of the ample material available, I want to recount the path I took through the maze of arguments, pro and con, which led to the outcome of this mental and spiritual journey.

1

Surprised!

★ ★ ★

I have seven daughters.

Frequently when I was a guest speaker, the person presenting me would single out this fact from my biographical sheet, and save it for final mention in his introduction. How often I have heard the words, "Our speaker is the father of seven girls."

And how often I have walked to the pulpit amidst the "oh's" and "ah's" to respond, "With all those women in my house, I was always happy for even a 'male'-box out front."

At college chapels I went through a longer routine: "I feel right at home here. You see... I live in a girls' dormitory."

When the mild laughter died down, I would comment, "I'm the dean of women." More laughter. Then, "I was once introduced as 'Father Flinnigan from

Girl's Town.'" More laughter. Then my final line: "After seven girls, if we ever have a little boy, we already have a name picked out for him — Henry the Eighth." The loud laughter at this quip indicated good rapport with my college audience.

With seven daughters, I have often thought, "I'll never have a son in the ministry." Never did I dream that I might have a daughter following in the same calling, especially since all seven were married and successfully pursuing secular vocations. But I was in for a big surprise.

The bombshell fell during a routine phone call in the spring of 1988. My wife, who faithfully keeps in touch with all of our daughters, dialed our second girl in upstate New York for a little chat. Her husband said that Janna, out at the moment, would call us on her return. When I came on the line to say "hi," he casually broke the news: "Are you aware that your daughter wants to become a minister?"

I was astounded. "You mean... she wants to be a preacher, the pastor of a church?" His answer softened my surprise. "I don't think she wants to do the preaching. I think she's more interested in counselling and educational ministries."

However, a few weeks later, stopping overnight on a business trip to New York City, our son-in-law set the record straight. "Janna says she wants to preach and pastor."

Part of my surprise stemmed from Janna's gentle nature and mild manner. It was difficult to visualize her pounding the pulpit and running a church.

Besides, now in her late thirties, she had been successful in the commercial world, most recently helping a business associate launch a new company.

But what caused my strongest reaction was the
recollection that women preachers were not always
well-accepted. Although she belonged to a denomination that practiced the ordination of women, I
knew that women preachers often had limited
approval and fought an up-hill battle for congregational acceptance.

In addition, I had been raised in a tradition that
frowned on women-pastors. Then, for forty years I
pastored a church whose denomination had voted
three times in favor of statements that were disapproving of women-pastors. For example, in its annual meeting in 1975, the Conservative Baptist Association of America, while recognizing the significant
contribution of women to the service of Christ and
encouraging women to use their spiritual gifts on
boards and committees, passed a resolution "that we
affirm the Biblical principle and pattern of the Christian ministry, as outlined in the Pauline epistles in
that the office of pastor-teacher remain the God-
given responsibility of men of God."

Janna was our second daughter, born in 1949,
six weeks after I began a 40-year ministry in Nanuet,
New York, 40 miles northwest of New York City.
From the beginning, she displayed firm resolve and
self-discipline. As a child, she practised her violin
early each morning. (Is there anything so melodious
as the screeching of a violin in the hands of a novice

at 6 a.m.?) To this day, she runs five miles several days a week, and for years she has kept her weight around the 100-pound mark.

Growing up, Janna participated in all church activities. At age 15, she waited tables at Montrose Summer Bible Conference in Pennsylvania. The next summer she was helper to a family out on Long Island, taking care of several children and cleaning house. Another summer she worked at a camp run by one of her high-school teachers where she met another worker, Gene, whom she married four days after her graduation from Wheaton College (Illinois) in June 1971. Their first son, Christopher, lived only six weeks. They have another boy, Jeremy, now a teenager.

Both she and her husband taught school for a while. When Gene became an executive with the Boy Scouts in the Syracuse, New York area, Janna went into the temporary office-help business, rising to office-manager. Gene became Director of Career Development at Hamilton College, and enrolled in a graduate program at Syracuse University. When he had completed his class work and was soon to earn his doctorate (receiving his Ed.D. in Adult Education in 1990), Janna made known her wish to go to seminary. Gene, easygoing and genial, commented, "She helped put me through graduate school. Now it's my turn to help her through seminary."

Wherever located, they always sought a church in which they could serve. They found a special church-home in the United Church of Christ in Bayberry, a suburb of Liverpool, New York. During their years of interaction with the pastor and people, Janna came to the conviction that the Lord was calling her into the ministry. The United Church of Christ denomination requires anyone wishing to be considered as a candidate for seminary to apply to his or her local church for an interview with the church council or a designated committee.

I wondered about Janna's motivations to go to seminary. Were they sparked by the feminist movement? Were they the product of women's lib? I found such conjectures groundless, however, when I read a copy of her letter of application to her home church which explained her reasoning. Dated January 4, 1988, it said, in part:

"During the last eight years, the people and programs at Bayberry have impacted my life in numerous ways. Because of the acceptance I have experienced, the opportunities for growth the church has provided, and the counsel I have received from Dan and Jennifer [pastor and associate pastor], *I have come to the belief that God is leading me to seminary.*

"Deciding to respond to this call is not a decision that I have made lightly or hastily. Divinity school is not a direction I would choose for myself; however, I have the conviction that it is only in attending seminary that I can receive the training to find the life I am called to live.

"My plans are to enroll in Colgate-Rochester Divinity School as a full-time student either September 1988 or January 1989 (depending on when my husband completes his dissertation)."

Along with her application, Janna included the required "Personal Statement," quoted here in its entirety.

"'If you can stay out, stay out.' That is the advice my minister-father gives to potential candidates for ministry. For forty years I have been able to 'stay out' but recently have come to a point in my journey of faith when this is no longer feasible. In gentle and undramatic ways, I began to experience indications that if I were to find the life I was called to live for God, I would need to engage in full-time ministry.

"This was a gradual process which began six or seven years ago after our family relocated to Syracuse and began attending the United Church of Christ in Bayberry. I became very involved. Responding to the need for personal growth and additional study, I was accepted in the Lay Ministry program. The more time I dedicated to seeking God's Spirit in my personal life and church activities, the greater my hunger for spiritual food. I felt claimed by God and sought to find how He wanted me to live this life. I began to experience what I felt were indications of His guidance. Some results were professional and some were spiritual. I accepted a position to start up a new company for a business associate and I sought application in the Lay Ministry program. I perceived these activities as investing my gifts with God's Spirit and continuing on the road to finding what I was born for.

"I realized I was on a journey. Daily I had to be open to discerning God's will, determining where He was leading and choosing or not choosing to go along.

I can't pinpoint the time or circumstances but there were stirrings in me indicating I still hadn't found my vocation I was called to claim. The sense that I was called to full-time ministry was born. I have tried to deny this call but have learned as someone once said that 'No noise is so emphatic as the one you are trying not to listen to.' The tapping on my shoulder has not ceased.

"Realizing I would have to respond to this call, I attended the Conference on Ministry last November at Colgate-Rochester Divinity School. I came away from the experience with a sense that this seminary would be the right place for me. The spirit of community I experienced and the opportunity to be exposed to a variety of viewpoints resulted in a feeling that attending this school would equip me with the training to find the life I was called to live. I am ready to answer the call I have experienced.

"I sincerely believe that my past vocations and avocations have been providing me with experiences and skills necessary to pursue the ministry. I grew up in a parsonage and spent many hours in church-related activities and services. This experience has furnished me with a solid background in the Bible and church operations. Teaching school, being a parent and most recently managing a business have provided me with experience and skills in dealing with people. One of my frustrations with the business world was the lack of freedom to bring the Word of God into human interactions to aid others in dealing with life's struggles. I truly believe that unless we as

individuals, a society or a church, are open to the mystery of God and attempt to interpret and articulate the possibilities of God's love for others, our lives will not be fulfilling.

"In my life I have been privileged to have been exposed to some very special people. They empowered me to use my abilities. I believe that all believers, and especially ministers, should live with the profound sense of the responsibility to be cultivators, enabling others to be more than they deemed possible with the assistance of God's Spirit. Reflecting God's Word and God's perspective, Christian ministry is articulating the possibilities of God's love in every situation.

"At this time I am unclear into what specific area of service I am being called. As He has in the past, I am confident if I am open to His leading, God will guide me to find the life I was called to live."

Janna's pastor of nine years wrote a letter of commendation, stating that her sincerity and dedication as a church member and as a person were unquestionable. He listed the many ways she had served: as a deacon, visiting shut-in members, leading several small groups, chairing the membership committee as well as the Deacon Care Program, and at that time fulfilling the role of Vice-Moderator of the congregation which required heading up the Program Planning Committee, the nominating process and the Renewal Committee.

He wrote, *"When she has led a worship service for the Women's Retreat or preached a sermon to the whole congregation, I have received only positive reports, such as how inspirational she was. She presents herself well in front of a group. She is an active member of the Lay Ministry Program of the New York Conference. I believe she has completed all of her reading assignments ahead of time.*

"Janna's great strength is in organization. Working under goals and deadlines, she accomplishes virtually any task she accepts.

"I have no reservations in my recommendation of Janna as a Candidate for the Christian Ministry."

Janna entered seminary in the fall of 1988, enrolling in a three-year ministerial course. Her motivation was not to demand equality with the masculine world. She was not gunning for women's rights. Her aim was not to escape the kitchen, break free from the narrow roles of tradition, re-structure society, achieve equal pay for equal work, nor to topple male domination. Rather, she had sensed the call of God.

She was no crusader. In fact, it was difficult to picture her in the pulpit — this petite, pretty, 5'3", trim, soft-spoken person. Since her full name is Janna Joy (Flynn) Roche, perhaps I could say that I was indeed "surprised by Joy."

But when the surprise wore off, I realized that I would have to face the question of women preachers and pastors. With all the interest on the subject, naturally I was aware of the issue and of the prevailing opposition in my circles to woman clergy, but I had never given the matter major attention. Now I would have to do so.

But where would I begin? Years before, I had set up a folder in my files titled, "Women in Ministry," into which I had tossed pertinent articles and book references. This file was now quite thick because scholars had been producing more and more literature on both sides of the controversy. I decided to begin my intellectual and spiritual journey by sorting through the material in this folder.

2

Sampling My File on Woman's Role

★ ★ ★

The phone call announcing Janna's intention to study for the ministry came in the spring of 1988. The following September, she enrolled as a full-time student in Colgate-Rochester Divinity School in Rochester, New York. In the intervening months, I sorted through the material in my folder, "Women in Ministry."

In 1958 when Charles C. Ryrie wrote his book, *The Place of Women in the Church* (Macmillan), four publishers rejected the manuscript because the subject was not relevant. At that time I had no folder, "Women in Ministry." I'm not sure when I started this file, probably in the early '60's. Now, in 1988, I found a thick folder to review.

What would I find? Would the material support the viewpoint in which I had been reared — that women should stay out of the pulpit? Or would I discover sound argumentation for women preachers and pastors? Would it be subordination or ordination? Or as someone phrased the two positions, Adam's rib or women's lib?

A few facts soon became apparent. First, good and scholarly people stood on both sides of the issue. Often professors on the same seminary faculty held opposite views. Though today many evangelical denominations do not believe in women-pastors, I learned that leading evangelical figures of an earlier era, like D.L. Moody and A.J. Gordon, and self-avowed fundamentalists like W.B. Riley and J.R. Straton (former pastor of New York City's Calvary Baptist Church), saw their support of women preachers as compatible with biblical literalism.

A second fact stood out. Because of increasing interest in the topic, the literature had proliferated in recent years, not only in quantity but in academic sophistication. I learned that Calvin College's library gained over 2,000 titles in gender studies in one four-year period.

Still another fact — the feminist position seemed to be gaining favor. Here was an issue that would not go away, and one on which I would have to make a decision.

It would be impossible to summarize all the articles, clippings and findings from related book-reading which I found in my folder. So what I have done in the rest of this chapter is to select miscellaneous references which, though they may seem to be a hodge podge without rhyme or reason, struck me as having significant interest to a father who had recently learned of his daughter's call to the ministry. Instead of arranging the material in any logical manner, I present it in chronological sequence, according to the year of publication, and thus in the order in which the items came across my desk, entered my thinking and became part of the input that would ultimately help me reach my verdict.

The first reference goes back to well over a century ago.

1859. In a booklet first published in 1859, I found a quote from Catherine Booth, co-founder of the Salvation Army, who, despite much opposition, broke into the male-dominated ranks of preachers. She wrote that "judging from the blessed results which have almost invariably followed the ministrations of women in the cause of Christ, we fear it will be found in the great day of account that a mistaken and unjustifiable application of the passage, *Let your women keep silence in the churches,* has resulted in more loss to the Church, evil to the world and dishonor to God...." (*Female Ministry or Women's Right to Preach The Gospel*, London: Morgan & Chase, 1859, reprinted 1975 by the Salvation Army, New York, p. 20).

1941. Taking the opposite position, John R. Rice made this strong statement: "Feminism in the churches is a blight that has grieved God and has made ineffectual His power.... I have no doubt that millions will go to Hell because of the unscriptural practice of women preachers" (*Bobbed Hair, Bossy Wives, and Women Preachers*, Murfreesboro: Sword of the Lord, p. 59).

1949. My favorite professor at Moody Bible Institute, Dr. P.B. Fitzwater, affirmed that a woman "may be... instructor of men... in short, in whatever she has ability for, except a pastoral head" (*Women: Her Mission, Position, and Ministry*, Grand Rapids: Wm. B. Eerdmans Publishing Co., p. 66).

1958. Charles C. Ryrie, in his book referred to earlier, took a view much narrower than Fitzwater's. He concluded that "the early church did not make a practice of permitting women to speak in their public meetings" (p. 78). Ryrie did not deny that women may have prophesied and prayed, but suggested that the practice was exceptional and limited to the church at Corinth, a city of very loose standards.

1973. The July-August issue of the magazine, *The Other Side*, was devoted completely to urging a higher role of women in Christian ministry. One article pointed out that we have been conditioned to accept traditional ideas as to what is masculine or feminine. Boys are to play rough and not cry, whereas girls are to be dainty and wear ruffles. Men become lawyers, machinists or doctors. Girls become mothers and homemakers, perhaps working out of the home as secretaries or nurses. This carries into church life where the men are to be pastors, and the women in charge of the kitchen or teaching the children.

The article also pointed out that concepts of masculinity and femininity vary from culture to culture.

In one New Guinea tribe, it was considered ideal for women to have an aggressive, dominant disposition and men to have a sensitive, emotionally-dependent temperament. Conclusion: Even if differences do exist between the sexes, why should they keep a woman from being and doing what she wants to be and do as a human being?

1974. A clipping from a Monday edition of the *New York Times* reported an incredible incident in an Episcopal church in downtown New York City the day before. An ordained deaconess, distributing communion to people in line, came to a man who, unknown to her, violently opposed women clergy. After receiving communion, he deliberately and sharply raked his fingernails across the back of her hand, drawing blood. Then he uttered a vicious insult, confirming his hatred.

Also 1974. *Moody Monthly* (February) warned in an article, "What's Behind the Equal Rights Amendment?" that ERA's implications went far beyond guaranteeing equal pay for equal work, and would affect our society much more drastically. Evangelicals pointed out, however, that since women do experience economic inequality in many areas, it was possible to be against ERA while still supporting justice for women. Opponents of ERA quipped that they favored the E and the R, but not the A.

1975. This was one of the years that my own denomination, Conservative Baptists, went on record at their annual convention to affirm that the office of pastor-teacher should be reserved for men, though at the same time encouraging the involvement of women in Christian service in keeping with their spiritual gifts. Similar resolutions were passed in 1978 and 1986.

Also 1975. After a well-known woman author wrote on "Why I Oppose the Ordination of Women" in *Christianity Today* (June 6), a letter to the editor in the July 18 issue commented that "women who so forcefully express opinions on the role of women in the church as only submissive, in effect contradict their own assertions. If Paul was right when he said women should remain silent and not be allowed to speak 'in church,' then by what authority do they write? To be silent in church would surely include not speaking out publicly in a church journal such as *Christianity Today!*"

Also 1975. This year saw the publication of Paul Jewett's book, *Man as Male and Female* (Eerdmans), which is considered one of the classics in support of the egalitarian view. It claims that the fullness of the image of God in man required the creation of both male and female. Jewett argued that Paul, as a hangover from his rabbinical background, taught that women should be subordinate to men, but then, influenced by the implications of the gospel, later abolished the gender hierarchy and taught the equality of the sexes, especially in Galatians 3:28. But critics cite Jewett's acceptance of a contradiction in Paul as a flaw in Jewett's theory of inspiration.

1976. A *Christianity Today* editorial (January 2) warned against the increasing efforts to rewrite the

Bible, the creeds and the hymns of the church for the purpose of neutralizing or abandoning what has been termed "sexist language." Critics of traditional translations suggested that the so-called masculine imagery of God as "father" and Jesus as "son" should be changed to include female symbols of "mother" and "daughter."

The writer pointed out that Bible translators and theologians have labored long and hard to determine what the writers of Scripture said and meant. To call Him "daughter" instead of "son" downgrades the written Word by overriding the fact that God chose to reveal Himself as man. Jesus was not a woman. Maintaining the masculinity of Jesus in no way cancels out the rightful status of women. Feminine claim for full personhood need not alter what God has written. The editorial ended with the plea to let God be God and man be man.

At a service in which God was addressed as "mother" in the prayers and liturgy, one female seminary graduate commented, "The God they were worshiping is not the God I know."

Around this time, I jotted down some quips involving sexist language. For example, instead of HIStory, should we talk about HERstory? Why do we call the feminine operation HYSterectomy? Should it not be HERterectomy? Will the mailman be known as the person-person? How would ladies like it if the oft-used excuse were changed to say, "The Devil made me do it. Yes, SHE did"? How about, "Everybody owns a VCR, every Tom, Dick and Harriet"?

1977. A popular magazine related how on Saturday, January 8, 1977, almost 500 people crowded into the quiet, small sanctuary of St. John's Episcopal Church in Crawfordsville, Indiana, which normally accommodated only 125 people. Many came from as far away as California and Florida to witness a special ceremony. Also present were two of the sheriff's armed deputies, reasonably unobtrusive in plain clothes, yet obviously watching the congregation carefully. Why should the ordination ceremony of an Episcopal priest require the presence of two armed men? The only reason was the fact that the priest to be ordained was a woman.

Natalia Vonnegut, mother of four, was to become that afternoon the second woman Episcopal priest in Indiana, and the fourth regularly ordained woman Episcopal priest in the United States. For over a month, she had been receiving threatening phone calls. Just the previous night an unidentified male voice had warned, "If you care anything about the welfare of your children, you won't go through with the ordination ceremony."

The ordination service proceeded without incident and the threats never materialized. A totally expected protest to the proceedings occurred when the officiating priest recited the question that precedes all Episcopal ordinations, "If any know any impediment or crime because of which we should not proceed, come forward now and make it known." One male stood to represent an Episcopalian organization opposed to female priests. He called the proceedings "sacrilegious" and "heresy." To ordain women could only result in schism from the true body of Christ. As the man turned and left the church, the ordination continued (Elizabeth Rodgers Dobell, "God And Woman: The Hidden History," *Redbook Magazine*, March 1978, p. 38).

1978. "Women in Executive Role" was the topic of the *Christian Leadership Letter*, a monthly publication of World Vision edited by Ted W. Engstrom and Edward R. Dayton. The authors reminded us that women missionaries have been "outstanding in their zeal and in their leadership. They have preached, planted churches, administered programs and done practically everything that their male counterparts have done." Then they made an interesting aside: "It is worth wondering why some Western churches have had so much trouble in accepting women in roles of leadership when they have been exercising all of these gifts overseas!"

But, continued the article, in our country many Christian organizations are heavily weighted with women in low paying clerical jobs, and few in executive positions. The editors believed it was time for a change and suggested that executives look at their current staff, note those with latent managerial gifts, arrange for their training, offer them new responsibilities and reward them with promotions. The editors often found in their management seminars that the person scoring highest on their supervisory skills test was a woman.

They ended the letter, "Women need the encouragement and support of men (and other women) to become all that God would have them to be. They need to be accepted as equal business associates and as individuals who can think knowledgeably and perform effectively. Given the opportunity, there are many women who would surprise themselves, as well as their fellow workers, at how well they might carry out an executive position" (919 W. Huntington Drive, Monrovia, CA, 91016, USA, September).

1980. *Eternity Magazine* (December), in an article titled, "Paul, Women, and the Church," displayed a chart showing how fifteen modern interpreters understood the following five key Bible passages:

- 1 Corinthians 11:3-9 which includes the phrase, *the head of the woman is man.*
- 1 Corinthians 14:33-35 which speaks about women being silent in the churches.
- Galatians 3:26-29 which says that in Christ there is neither male nor female.
- Ephesians 5:21-24 which instructs wives to submit to their husbands.
- 1 Timothy 2:11-15 which says women are not to teach nor have authority over men.

The interpretations of these fifteen authors were placed toward the left or right of the chart to represent their relatively liberal or conservative character. Interestingly, though all interpreters honored the Bible as God's inspired Word, they differed in their understanding of the texts. In fact, the same Scriptures, which according to some interpreters taught that women should be silent and without authority in the church, were understood by other authors to mean just the opposite, as not denying the right of women to speak in the church except under certain circumstances. It was evident that equally educated scholars, equally evangelical, could reach differing conclusions on not-so-clear passages.

1981. *Christianity Today* ran parallel articles, "The Ordination of Women: Yes," and "No" (February 20).

This was the year Sandra Day O'Connor was appointed to the US Supreme Court. An article noted that women have often held high national positions with distinction, such as Golda Meir, Israeli Prime Minister, and Margaret Thatcher, formidable Prime Minister of Great Britain. Someone pointed out that though Thatcher could lead a great Western power with its millions of citizens, as a woman she could not serve as leader in many of our evangelical churches. Other nations with recent female heads include the Philippines, Pakistan, Iceland and India.

1982. The fifth Evangelical Women's Caucus (begun in 1974 as an offshoot of Evangelicals for Social Action) met for four days in July in Seattle, Washington. Over 700 men and women met to address the concerns of the Christian feminist. At the Communion service, women led, preached and served. Behind the loaves of bread and pitchers of grape juice sat several women pastors. Above the altar hung a banner that said, *How happy is she who has had faith that the Lord's promise would be fulfilled* (Luke 1:45).

One woman Presbyterian pastor present said, "Women pastors are judged a lot more on their appearance than men are. People have the sexual imagery-in-the pulpit problem. You have to have a gentleness, but a thick armor." Said another female pastor, "I always feel I have to justify my sense of God's call to the ministry twenty times more than a man does."

A male musician appearing at the conference said that since he had taken a stand with Christian feminism in the past five years, invitations to sing at Christian gatherings had decreased. Christians were still sending disapproving mail.

1986. Another *Christianity Today* article posed the question, "Women in Seminary: Preparing for What?" (September 5). Thirty-four evangelical seminaries reported that during the previous two decades their percentage of female students had increased twice as fast as that of the total student population. The current census of these schools was nearly 20% female, up from less than 10% in 1965. (Today the percentage in evangelical seminaries is around 25%, whereas liberal schools run close to 50%).

Also 1986. Dallas Seminary admitted a woman to its master of theology program for the first time. Though the seminary's decision reflected their belief that leaders of women's ministries should receive a thorough Scriptural training, Dallas still held that women should not be ordained as senior pastors. A few years earlier, Western Conservative Baptist Seminary opened the Master of Divinity degree up to women with the understanding that they were not being trained to become senior pastors.

The article said that most women in seminary discover that seminary classes sharpen their knowledge of the Bible and their skill in handling it. But where will they go at graduation? Many are accepted as assistant and associate pastors in team ministries. Bishops and superintendents in some denominations have the power to prevent female ordinations in their jurisdictions. Clergy couples have become common with over one thousand pairs now serving denominations all over the nation. Hundreds of women serve as sole pastors but mostly in small, rural churches. They will have difficulty moving on to more responsible second and third positions. Women are not yet emerging as senior pastors in larger, multiple-staff situations, but rather they are still women in their first job with little or no prospect of advancement to more challenging locations — "all dressed up with no place to go."

The article ended with a statement from a woman seminarian, echoing the conviction of her colleagues: "I don't believe that God, who placed a call on my life, made a mistake." And a male seminary director said, "The church is impoverished to the extent that it fails to use the gifts God gives to women."

Right after reading this article, and just before my wife and I left for a seven-week trip to visit mission fields in Africa, I was dining with a leader in our denomination who had just come from his Wheaton office. I asked, "What's new in the evangelical world these days?" Unenthusiastically, he replied, "Dr. Kantzer, editor of *Christianity Today*, is coming out in favor of women's ordination in an October issue." On my return from Africa in early November, I read the sixteen-page report of Christianity Today Institute (Oct. 3, 1986) titled, "Women in Leadership: Finding Ways to Serve the Church."

The five articles dealt with all aspects of the issue. Authors included women church leaders and theological professors who summarized conflicting exegetical treatment of relevant biblical passages. The contributors were divided on the extent to which women should participate in church leadership. Many felt that women should be given greater opportunities but not be ordained. Others felt ordination provided women with a needed outlet for their genuine gifts of teaching, leadership and caring. Dr. Kantzer wrapped up the report by opting for the ordination of women.

Also 1986. Most of the papers delivered at the annual national conference of the Evangelical Theological Society at the end of 1986 dealt with the role of women in ministry. Roughly half of them adopted the hierarchical position, and the other half took the egalitarian side.

1987. A few months after Christianity Today Institute's report in which several authors advocated the ordination of women, *Moody Monthly* countered with a one-page piece, "Ordination Is Not for Women," by Dr. Gleason Archer, Professor at Trinity Evangelical Divinity School. (Two of the Christianity

Today Institute's pro-ordination articles were written by his colleagues at Trinity.) He said, "In 1 Timothy 2:11-13, Paul... says women must learn quietly in submission, and they are not permitted to teach men or exercise authority over them... To interpret 1 Timothy 2:13-14 to mean the very opposite of what it clearly says is to deviate from the authority of New Testament teaching. And to conclude that women may teach authoritatively as ordained pastors is to deviate from proper hermeneutics.... There is absolutely no reason to believe that Paul's prohibition is only cultural, limited to the women of a particular place and time. If teaching that is as simple and clear as this can be reinterpreted according to the moods and fashions of our day, then Paul's other inspired teachings may also be reinterpreted" (February, p. 8).

This was the last of the articles I added to my "Women in Ministry" folder before the phone call about Janna's decision to enter the ministry came. Never did I dream of how significant all this material would become to me personally, as I researched this theme. Not only would I have to re-read the books and articles, but I would also have to reach out to additional literature beyond my file. I wondered as to the outcome of my investigation.

When a man writes a book on women in ministry, women assume that male prejudice will govern his approach. Similarly, when a woman writes on the place of women in church leadership, men expect a feminist bias. But how will a father write — a pastor-father whose background and denomination oppose women preachers — when he discovers that his daughter claims a call to the ministry, and has enrolled in seminary to become a pastor? Which will prevail — fidelity to biblical teaching or loyalty to daughter?

3

Jesus And Women

★ ★ ★

Janna "hated" her first semester in seminary. Entering Colgate-Rochester in the fall of 1988, she found re-learning the disciplines of study and writing term papers an almost overwhelming change from the business world. But determined to survive, she began to enjoy school during her second semester and managed to get all A's or B's in her first-year courses. At thirty-nine, she felt right at home in a student body of two hundred whose median age was in the late thirties, fifty percent of whom were women, including many daughters of pastors.

Before seminary, she and her husband, Gene, sold their town house in Syracuse and moved to Clinton, New York, the location of Hamilton College where Gene is Director of Career Counseling. This enabled Gene and their son, Jeremy, to be together during the two days each week that Janna stayed at the seminary.

In February 1989, my church held a fortieth anniversary-retirement dinner for my wife and me. Janna, halfway through her first year, was chosen by her six sisters to represent them on the program. She capably delivered a well-prepared and humorously accurate picture of life with their minister-father.

Though she had given a couple of sermons in pre-seminary days during a lay ministry program, toward the end of her first year she received five or six invitations to preach, mainly in Presbyterian or United Church of Christ churches. On a trip in upstate New York in August, my wife and I dropped in at the Presbyterian church of Waterville and watched her lead the entire service, including a thoughtful twelve-minute message, "One Thing Is Needful," based on the story of Mary and Martha. Also, during the summer, she took an intensive five-day course at Hartford Seminary in Cincinatti on Effective Church Management.

During Janna's first year at seminary, I was naturally doing a lot of thinking about the role of women. I was impressed with the many references in my folder to the relationship Jesus had with women. So, I gave attention to this topic.

JESUS' TREATMENT SO DIFFERENT FROM CONTEMPORARY PRACTICE.

We take for granted the elevated position women have gained in our western culture. This makes it difficult to imagine how radical Jesus' attitude toward them must have seemed to His contemporaries. The writings of that era indicate a strongly negative attitude toward women. Yet not once in the Gospels does He humiliate a female. No word of deprecation ever falls from His lips. He denounces power-wielding men, but never rebukes a woman. He treats women as fully human, possessing value. He regards women as the equal of men. He does not lift women to the level of man, for He doesn't perceive people on levels, but accepts both men and women as persons. Both are sinners. Both need forgiveness. Both can understand spiritual truth. Both can approach Him with freedom. Both can become His followers. One writer says that in the four Gospels "there is a total of 633 verses in which Jesus refers to women, and almost none of these is negative in tone" (Mary Stewart Van Leeuwen, *Christianity Today*, July 16, 1990, p. 21). He was so remarkably supportive of womanhood that we can only conclude that He wanted to restore women to their position of dignity possessed before the Fall.

As I grasped the downtrodden condition of women in first-century Judaism, I began to better understand the upheaval His behavior brought to the scene. According to the rabbis, a man was not to talk to a woman in the street. A woman was inferior in all things to man. In court, a woman's testimony was not considered valid. Women did not count as members of the congregation. For a congregation to exist, it required at least ten men; nine men plus hundreds of women would not suffice. In the synagogue, women were required to sit separately from men. In the temple, they could approach no closer than the outer Court of the Women. Women's sphere was the domestic; consequently, she received no education. Women were regarded as property, first of their fathers, then of their husbands. A husband could divorce his wife at whim, but a wife could not divorce her husband. Men would pray every morning, "Blessed art Thou, O Lord, Who hast not made me a heathen, a slave, nor a woman." Men were considered superior; women, inferior. Men ruled; women obeyed. It was a man's world.

Against this background, Jesus' posture looms drastic — not so much by direct discussion, nor by attack on the status quo, but rather, by regally bypassing current conventions He disavowed the viewpoint of His people. By His amazing actions He demonstrated the dignity and equality of women in His realm.

LINEAGE AND INFANCY

Perhaps this new perspective is reflected in the first chapter of the New Testament. Generally, only male names were listed in Jewish genealogies, showing the non-status of women. The inclusion of four women in the lineage of Jesus in Matthew 1 grabs our attention. An astonishing change is about to take place in a society dominated by males. The Messiah will relate to women in an open and unheard of manner.

Also, perhaps the witness of a prophetess at the presentation of baby Jesus in the temple foreshadowed the equality of the sexes in His future ministry. Not only male Simeon, but also female Anna openly thanked God for the baby. This exercise by Anna did not differ from that of Simeon. It was essentially the same message in the same public place. She was not cloistered in some secluded nook, but rather spoke clearly to those assembled, probably at the hour of prayer. The spirit of prophecy was poured out as fully on the female as on the male.

The balance of the sexes often occurs in the Gospels: the song of Zachariah and the song of Mary; here, the praise of Simeon and Anna; the conversations with Nicodemus and the woman of Samaria; the confessions of Peter and Martha.

THE TEACHINGS OF JESUS

Though we do not have any record of Jesus ever giving a lecture on "Women in Today's Society," many of His teachings mirror women as honorable persons. He never spoke of them in derogatory stereotypes, but He accepted them as made in the image of God. To teach spiritual truth, Jesus alluded to women in Old Testament history like the Queen of Sheba (Luke 11:31) and the widow of Zarephath (Luke 4:25-26).

Seeing a widow toss two small coins inconspicuously into the temple treasury, He praised this poor female for giving more than all of the rich men with their large but meaningless gifts (Luke 21:1-4). Just before this incident, Jesus had condemned the rabbis for their hypocrisy in publicly offering long prayers, while privately robbing widows of their houses (Luke 20:45-47). Several times He demonstrated solidarity with widows, perhaps the most defenseless and poverty-stricken class in His day.

Jesus bluntly denounced the practice of allowing husbands to divorce their wives for trifling reasons, while denying the wife the right of divorce if unfairly treated by her husband (Matthew 19:9). He thereby seemed to assign women an equal standing with men in the social structure, as well as strongly implying that loyalty in marriage is the responsibility of both partners.

Jesus regarded women as significant subjects, not sexual objects. He warned that looking at a woman lustfully made a man guilty of mental adultery (Matthew 5:28). Though Jesus and the rabbis agreed on the sinfulness of lust, they disagreed on its inevitability. The rabbis held that the presence of a woman made lust unavoidable, so they called for the complete segregation of women. But Jesus believed that man was responsible for his own thought life, and could control his lust. Therefore, He allowed women to mix freely with His disciples. One of the charges brought against Jesus at His trial, according to an addition in Marcion's translation of Luke 23:2, was the attitude of Jesus toward women, plus the fact that a group of them followed Him. But had there been the slightest evidence of misconduct, the scandal would have been widely publicized, and His ministry disgraced.

In mingling openly with women, Jesus engaged them in theological dialogue. Whereas rabbis refused to teach women, holding that the law would better be burned than taught to a woman, Jesus instructed men and women alike.

Parables

Rabbinic parables purposely avoided mentioning women. But Jesus often drew materials from the everyday world of women. He spoke of a woman putting leaven in her bread (Matthew 13:33), of two men in the field at the Second Coming of Christ, followed immediately by mention of two women grinding at the mill (Matthew 24:40-41), of ten wedding attendants, five wise virgins and five foolish (Matthew 25:1), of a lowly housewife who swept her house to find a coin and rejoiced at her success, representing the Heavenly Father who searches for the lost and rejoices at their repentance (Luke 15:8-10) and of the persevering widow who kept bothering a heartless judge till he rendered justice (Luke 18:1-8). Thus, He intimates that women were not second-rate players in the game of life, but primary, consequential persons in their own right.

Miracles

Jesus did not confine His miracles to men. He healed Peter's mother-in-law (Matthew 8:14-15). He raised Jairus' daughter (Matthew 9:23-25). He healed the daughter of the Syrophenician woman, after an extended dialogue in which He talked with her as a person possessing intelligence and perception (Matthew 15:21-28).

Jesus showed compassion for the widow of Nain by raising her only son from the dead (Luke 7:11-17). He healed a woman in the synagogue who had been bent over for eighteen years, calling her a "daughter of Abraham" (Luke 13:10-17). "Son of Abraham" was a commonly used title, but "daughter of Abraham" was virtually unknown in Judaistic writing. By so calling her, Jesus implied a high value on womanhood.

Jesus healed a woman who for twelve years had suffered from an incurable hemorrhage (Luke 8:43-48). Barred from all religious services, separated from husband and family, forbidden to touch anyone, this outcast tried to find relief by pressing through the crowd towards Jesus, and secretly touching the hem of His garment. The typical religious leader of that day would have cursed the polluted woman and hurried away for ceremonial cleansing. But He, unconcerned that He had been touched by someone unclean, graciously sent her away in peace.

JESUS' TREATMENT OF SINFUL WOMEN

Although Jesus' attitude was revolutionary, women, like men, were sinners in need of salvation. Jesus did not shy away from extending His grace to immoral, but repentant, women.

The Samaritan Woman

The most celebrated occasion of Jesus dealing with a woman from the wrong side of the tracks was His conversation with the Samaritan woman (John 4:6-39). She had three strikes against her: she was a Samaritan; she was promiscuous; and she was a woman. However, He saw her as a person, dealt with her problem and respected her capacity to understand spiritual truth, including His "Messiahship." Her response was so enthusiastic that she evangelized the entire city — a woman missionary bringing many Samaritans to faith in Jesus.

The record says that the disciples, on returning from grocery shopping in the city, *marvelled that He talked with the woman* (vs. 27). His action was completely out of place in His culture, and a violation of rabbinical law. Jesus' love knows no boundaries of race, class or gender.

A Woman of the Street

Early in His Galilean ministry, Jesus was dining at the home of a Pharisee (Luke 7:36-50). At such meals, guests removed their sandals and reclined with their feet behind them. An uninvited guest, a notorious prostitute, learning that Jesus was there, walked in with a flask of perfume and acted very emotionally. Weeping tears onto His feet, then wiping them with her hair and kissing them, she anointed His feet with the perfume. Jesus, a young, unmarried man, allowed all this without embarrassment and without compliance with her life-style. Recognizing her desire for a new life, He commended her for her love and faith, telling her to go in peace. Perhaps He was the first man who had ever treated her as a person rather than a sex object. Jesus told his male host to profit from her example.

The Woman Caught in Adultery

One day Jesus' opponents tried to trap Him by bringing a woman, caught in the act of adultery, to Him to see if He would agree with the penalty of stoning laid down in Moses' law (John 8:1-11). Remarkably, they did not bring the male, although Moses had specifically passed the sentence of death on the adulterer as well as on the adulteress. Jesus not only dodged the snare, but turned the table on them with the challenge, *"He that is without sin among you, let him first cast a stone at her."* The woman waited. When all the men had slunk away, Jesus dismissed her with a blend of mercy and justice — no condemnation, but no more immorality. He elevated womanhood by exposing the double standard of these male scribes.

WOMEN AS DISCIPLES

Rabbis avoided the company of women as much as possible. But Jesus encouraged women to become His followers and join His band. Women sensed something different in the bearing of this man who, without impropriety, cut through the barricades of tradition.

Their ease in His presence explains the almost unbelievable fact that, along with the Twelve, a group of women disciples accompanied Him on some preaching missions. Luke makes a special point of giving some of their names. Speaking of Jesus' Galilean ministry throughout every city and village, he wrote, *The Twelve were with him, and also some women who had been cured of evil spirits and diseases; Mary (called Magdalene) from whom seven demons had come out; Joanna the wife of Cuza, the manager of Herod's household; Susanna; and many others. These women were helping to support them out of their own means* (Luke 8:1-3). These ladies provided a major source of financial income that made Jesus' itinerant ministry possible. One of them may have sewed Jesus' seamless tunic, "woven from the top throughout," a robe so valuable that the soldiers at the cross did not tear it into parts, but gambled for it.

Sometimes Jesus spent time alone with the inner three, other times with the Twelve, but Luke makes it clear that on many occasions women were present as well. An early church writer, Origen, mentioned that women accompanied the apostles into the wilderness, "forgetting the weakness of their sex and a regard for outward propriety in thus following their Teacher into the desert places" (Mary J. Evans, *Women in the Bible*, Downers Grove: InterVarsity, 1983, p. 50). Probably some single and some married, these women left home and family for periods of time to follow their Master, going not only the length and breadth of Galilee, but even to Jerusalem, remaining faithful to the end.

47

Mary and Martha

Naturally, many women whose responsibilities kept them from accompanying Jesus from place to place were deeply moved by His message. How could they understand the Old Testament law when rabbis refused to teach women? But Jesus taught women as well as men. Among such women were sisters, Mary and Martha, whose home He often visited when in the Jerusalem-Bethany area. Such visitation must have seemed incomprehensible to the religious leaders, for no rabbi would dream of entering a house where two sisters lived, much less conversing with them on spiritual matters. But Jesus' heavenly mandate took precedence over human custom. He fellowshiped with these women, showing the same respect to them as to His male followers.

Luke records an invitation to their home for dinner. While Martha prepared the meal, Mary sat at His feet. It's the picture of a rabbi instructing his pupil, incredibly a woman. When Martha complained to Jesus that Mary was not helping her, He rebuked Martha and commended Mary's decision.

The lesson was not lost on Martha. Whether or not she left the kitchen on this occasion to join Mary at the feet of Jesus, Martha did take the place of a disciple on other occasions. This became evident at the death of her brother, Lazarus, when she revealed understanding of lessons taught her (John 11:20-27). Jesus used the event to make a great affirmation, *"I am the resurrection, and the life"* (vs. 25).

Then Martha went to call Mary, using the significant title, *"The Teacher is here"* (vs. 31).

Mary may have been the most devoted pupil Jesus had. Though Martha was given understanding on the resurrection, Mary seems to have been the first to grasp the meaning of His death. At a dinner in Bethany not too many days before the crucifixion, Mary took it upon herself to do something unconventional. In an episode reminiscent of the prostitute's anointing of Jesus, Mary opened a vase of costly perfume, anointed Jesus and immodestly let down her hair to wipe His feet (John 12:1-8).

Her action must have frustrated the men at the dinner, and fostered Judas' criticism of her action as waste. Jesus immediately came to Mary's defense, indicating that she possessed far more discernment concerning His death than all of the others there. Jesus said that she did it to prepare Him for burial (Matthew 26:12). She saw that the forces of evil were closing in on her Master, sensed that He would soon die and realized that there might not be opportunity for a proper burial by loving hands, which turned out to be the case. So in advance of His death she gave His body a decent anointing. In recognition of her loving discernment, Jesus ordained the immortalization of her deed (vs. 13). Because Mary had sat at Jesus' feet, she, a woman, grasped what even the Twelve may have missed — the significance of the passion of Jesus.

WOMEN AT THE DEATH
AND RESURRECTION OF JESUS

One of Jesus' male followers betrayed Him. Another denied Him vehemently. All forsook Him and fled (Matthew 26:56). But the women who had followed Him all the way from Galilee were loyal to the end. They were joined by many other women along the way to Jerusalem (Mark 15:40,41). Along the via dolorosa they lamented Him. But even though weighed down with His cross and in pain from the scourging, Jesus had a word for them: *"Daughters of Jerusalem, weep not for me...."* (Luke 23:28). In His agony on the cross He made provision for one last widow, His own mother, entrusting her to John.

Many women watched the crucifixion "from afar." Anyone acquainted with the gruesome spectacle of a Roman execution understands why they kept their distance. They may well have risked their lives by their obvious loyalty, especially in following His body to the grave. They were present at its entombment, observing how His body was laid (Luke 23:55). They then left to prepare spices and ointments for a proper ministration which the arrival of the Sabbath had denied them.

Early on the first morning of the week, women could be seen wending their way toward the sepulchre. Beneath their almost inconsolable grief were hearts of love, courage and faith. What love! Last at the cross and first at the tomb. What courage! To think of entering a tomb sealed by Roman authority and guarded by soldiers. What faith! To roll away a stone so heavy it could be moved only by the combined efforts of several muscular men.

God rewarded their faithfulness. Women were the first to learn of His resurrection. Finding the stone rolled away, their perplexity turned to fear and amazement at the sight of an angel who said, "He is not here, but risen" (Matthew 28:1-6). Though Jewish law did not consider women's testimony admissible in court, Jesus entrusted the phenomenal news of the resurrection to women. In fact, many of the factual details related to His death, burial and resurrection became known through the eyewitness of women. Not only were women first to see the empty tomb and to hear the angel's announcement, but they were the first to gaze upon the risen Savior. He appeared first to Mary Magdalene (Mark 16:9). Then He appeared to women leaving the tomb (Matthew 28:9). It was not the Twelve who were the first to see the risen Savior; rather women were given precedence over the apostles at this momentous occurrence. Not only were women chosen as witnesses to the resurrection, but they were commissioned by the angel to "Go quickly, and tell His disciples." They became the initial announcers of the thrilling news. Though at first their message sounded like idle tales to the disciples, the fact that the news had been transmitted by women provided no excuse for male unbelief.

Does this teach something about the legitimacy of women as carriers of the gospel? Would Jesus have chosen women to publish the thrilling message, only to muzzle them later so they could not be announcers in the church of the good news?

NO WOMEN AMONG THE TWELVE

As highly as Jesus regarded women, He never took the ultimate step of choosing a woman apostle. If He intended to highlight the equality of women, why did He not show that women were eligible for equal ministries by appointing at least one woman among the Twelve? He spent the entire night in prayer before selecting His apostles. Yet Jesus did not choose a woman. Neither did those in the Upper Room choose a woman as the successor to Judas, although women were present, some of whom undoubtedly fulfilled the qualifications for apostleship listed at voting time by Peter (Acts 1:15-26).

Unlike the Twelve, the women that followed Jesus did not receive a special call. Choosing a woman apostle was Jesus' opportunity to graphically demonstrate His position on "women in ministry." But He did not take that step. Not one received the Master's ordination. As I continued my deliberation on my daughter's decision to enter the ministry, I knew that sometime I would have to face the problem of why there were no women among the Twelve.

I also wondered if Jesus' positive view of womanhood would carry over into the early church. Would women be honored and allowed places of ministry in their local fellowships?

4

Women
in the Early Church

★ ★ ★

The following event may be the first of its kind, eligible for the Guiness Book of World Records. On Sunday, June 3, 1990, I spoke in the morning service of the Immanuel Baptist Church of New Hartford, New York, an engagement I had accepted nearly a year in advance. On the same morning of the same day in the same town at the same hour, my daughter spoke at the New Hartford Presbyterian Church. Though close friends knew of this coincidence, the two congregations were unaware of the simultaneous father-and-daughter sermonic presentations not many blocks apart. As part of her practical-ministry requirement, Janna was serving an internship as Pastoral Assistant at this Presbyterian Church during her second year of seminary. There she regularly shared in leading the services,

occasionally team-preaching with the pastor. As the
year ended, she was invited to give the morning sermon. The Sunday happened to be the same day I
was scheduled for the Baptist Church in the same
town. My wife had a tough time deciding which
preacher to go hear. Ultimately she opted for me,
realizing that I was the one she had to live with after-
wards. Incidentally, the church invited Janna to
become their full-time Assistant Pastor, starting the
following fall, but she turned the offer down to finish
her final year of schooling.

My amusement at finding my daughter preaching
the same morning in the same city served to accel-
erate my deliberations on "women preachers." I had
seen how radically Jesus treated women during His
earthly ministry. Without male ego to defend, He
never put them down, nor ever rebuffed any with,
"Why don't you act like a woman?" Instead, going
directly against the current culture, He accepted
them as persons in their own right, and as equals
with men. I now wondered if Jesus' attitude toward
women carried over into the New Testament church.
Did the pioneers of the early church revert to the status quo and relegate women to a place of inferiority,
or did they regard them highly and allow them
important roles in ministry?

So I looked at the various churches mentioned in
the book of Acts, and at the epistles to these churches, to see what part women played in early church life.
The churches will be listed in the chronological order
of their appearance in the New Testament record.

THE CHURCH AT JERUSALEM

The first New Testament church was founded on the Day of Pentecost at Jerusalem as recorded in the opening two chapters of Acts. Significantly, women are alluded to in both chapters. The nucleus of the primitive church, which numbered about one hundred and twenty, assembled continuously during the ten days following the Ascension of Jesus to pray and wait for the coming of the promised Spirit. Women are specifically mentioned as members of the group (Acts 1:14). Women praying alongside men apparently posed no problem. This same group, men and women, were together on the Day of Pentecost when a rushing wind surrounded all of them, and flaming tongues rested on every one. Females, as well as males, were filled with the Spirit and began speaking in foreign languages (Acts 2:1-4).

Peter explained that the apostles were not drunk, but rather experiencing the long-waited promise of the Spirit. God had promised, *"I will pour out of my Spirit upon all flesh: and your sons and your daughters shall prophesy.... And on my servants and on my handmaidens I will pour out in those days of my Spirit; and they shall prophesy"* (Acts 2:15-18). Whatever other fulfillment this prediction may entail, it seems plain that God, according to His Word, poured out His Spirit upon believers — both men and women — to enable them to prophesy. And that's what the one hundred and twenty did, including women. The prophesying was not confined to fore-telling events, but involved the forth-telling to all their hearers the glad tidings of salvation through Christ with the invitation that *"whosoever shall call on the name of the Lord shall be saved"* (vs. 21).

Though some commentators suggest that women with the gift of prophecy should not use it in public, God said through the prophet Joel that daughters would exercise it in the same way as sons. Peter's adoption of Joel's prophecy as the inaugural statement at the birth of the church showed that the gift of God's Spirit for a prophetic ministry has been bestowed equally on women and men.

The three thousand who were baptized consisted of both men and women with no distinction between them. This was a switch from the custom of counting only men. For example, the feeding of the five thousand referred to the number of men only; women and children were not tallied (Matthew 14:21; John 6:10). But after Pentecost, women were counted on Jerusalem church records. Luke records of the growing church, *And believers were the more added to the Lord, multitudes both of men and women* (Acts 5:14).

Husband and wife, Ananias and Sapphira, pretended to bring a bigger offering than they actually gave. Both were struck dead. Church discipline applied to women and men alike (Acts 5:1-10).

When the Twelve saw the need for appointing overseers for alms distribution to needy widows, the entire congregation, both men and women, voted on the seven men (Acts 6:1-6). (I wondered: When women outnumber men in a church with a congregational form of government, does not the authority in that church really reside with the women?)

Mary, Mark's mother, opened her home as one of the meeting places of the church at Jerusalem, using her assets for the Lord. Many scholars think the upper room was in her home. It was to Mary's place that Peter gravitated on his miraculous release from prison, and there that he found an all-night prayer meeting in progress (Acts 12:1-17).

Obviously, the Twelve were clearly the leaders of the church at Jerusalem, succeeded by James. But women were accepted into full church membership in a manner foreign to current synagogue practice, sharing in prayer, prophecy, voting and discipline.

THE CHURCH AT SAMARIA

When persecution scattered the church of Jerusalem, "deacon" Philip journeyed to the city of Samaria where he led a great evangelistic effort. People listened, believed and were baptized. Luke adds, *both men and women* (Acts 8:12).

THE CHURCH AT JOPPA

Luke records the raising from the dead of a woman disciple named Dorcas, known for her good deeds. At her death, hearing that Peter was nearby, the saints at Joppa sent messengers to ask him to come. When Peter was ushered into the room where

Dorcas was laid out, weeping widows showed him the clothes which she had sewn for them in their poverty. Then through divine power, Peter presented her alive to *the saints and widows* (Acts 9:41). The name of this godly seamstress has not only been memorialized in Holy Writ, but also in the numerous DORCAS societies where church women sew for the needy.

I couldn't recall any similar miracle recorded of any saintly man in the early church.

THE CHURCH AT PHILIPPI

In a vision on his second missionary journey, Paul saw a man of Macedonia beseeching him to *come over into Macedonia, and help us* (Acts 16:9). Paul and his team traveled to Philippi, chief city of Macedonia, to hunt for the man, who turned out to be a woman, who held the key to the evangelizing of the city. A group of women, not qualified under Judaistic law to start a synagogue, met each sabbath beside a river to pray. Businesswoman Lydia became the first convert. Baptized along with her household, she opened her home as a meeting-place. She and her praying women-friends formed the nucleus of what may have been the first church in Europe. At the start, the small congregation may have looked to Lydia for leadership. The church began to grow, first with the addition of the slave girl who was dramatically healed of her demon possession. Jailed and beaten, Paul was able to lead the jailer and his family to faith in Christ, adding yet more to the church.

Very loyal to Paul, the church repeatedly sent offerings to support his ministry. In one of these thank you letters, Paul had the unpleasant task of trying to reconcile two leading ladies who for some unknown reason had been at odds. Paul called them both by name, Euodias and Syntyche (sometimes dubbed Mrs. Odious and Mrs. Soon-touchy), urging them to patch up their differences. It must have been a jolt when the letter was read publicly. But Paul also called them *those women which labored with me in the gospel....* (Philippians 4:3). He reminded them of past teamwork, not only with each other, but also with Paul. These two women had played an important part in the preaching of the gospel, far in excess of just material assistance. Their position of influence in the church gained from their past record of service made their present conflict a grave danger to the well-being of the church. Thus Paul's plea, "Ladies, get your act together."

We can be thankful for their disagreement; otherwise we would not have known of the significant contribution of these feminine Christian workers whose names were in the book of life. Of the four people mentioned by name in this epistle as workers at Philippi, two are men and two are women. The two men are Clement and Epaphroditus (Philippians 4:3,18). I could see no indication of any restriction on women's role, nor of any difference in status or function between males and females in the Philippian church.

THE CHURCH AT THESSALONICA

After Paul's preaching for three sabbaths in the synagogue at Thessalonica, several believed. Later, the church became the recipient of two New Testament Pauline epistles. Original believers included a great multitude of Greeks and *of the chief women not a few* (Acts 17:4).

AT ATHENS

Later, Paul traveled to Athens where he preached to the sophisticated philosophers on Mars Hill. We have no record of any church established in Athens, nor do we have any epistle written to them. But we do know that among the few converts was *a woman named Damaris* (Acts 17:34). Mentioned in the same sentence as Dionysius, a member of Court of Areopagus, she may have been an important citizen.

THE CHURCH AT CORINTH

Next stop was Corinth where, after early opposition, Paul had a successful eighteen-month stay. From his first letter to the Corinthian church, we know that no distinction was made between men and women participating in the service. Men prayed and spoke prophetically (1 Corinthians 11:4), and women prayed and spoke prophetically (vs. 5). Gifts are bestowed, not according to gender, but according to the sovereign choice of the Spirit (1 Corinthians 12:11).

In 1 Corinthians 7, Paul indicates that though marriage is honorable, under certain circumstances, voluntarily choosing to remain single may enable both men and women to devote all their care and service to God. The fact that Paul speaks specifically of the advantage of the unmarried woman over a wife in regard to ministry, seems to suggest that he presupposes the possibility of a full-time Christian career for women (vs. 32-35).

However, in this same epistle, Paul seems to contradict the practice of women praying and prophesying in the church service. He wrote the oft-repeated dictum, *Let your women keep silence in the churches: for it is not permitted unto them to speak* (1 Corinthians 14:34). I knew that I would have to face this apparent conflict as I thought about my daughter's intent to enter the ministry.

THE CHURCH AT EPHESUS

At Corinth, Paul met Priscilla and Aquila, a couple from Rome, through their mutual occupation of tent-making. The couple invited the apostle to stay in their home, and helped him in his fruitful church-planting enterprise. Realizing their value, Paul took them to Ephesus to nourish a work there until he could return from celebrating the Passover at Jerusalem. In Ephesus, Priscilla and Aquila opened their home for worship. Paul later wrote to the Corinthians from Ephesus saying, *Aquila and Priscilla greet you warmly in the Lord, and so does the church that meets at their house* (1 Corinthians 16:19, NIV).

Before Paul rejoined them after his Jerusalem jaunt, a certain Jew, Apollos, eloquent and mighty in the Scriptures, came to Ephesus and taught diligently in the synagogue. Checking him out, Priscilla and Aquila detected a defect in his teaching. The couple made opportunity to expound *unto him the way of God more perfectly* (Acts 18:26). Apollos humbly learned all he could, and then, fully informed in gospel truth, was sent to help out the church they had so recently left at Corinth.

Never mentioned separately, Priscilla and Aquila operated as a husband and wife team. But the wife seems to have been the more prominent of the two. Priscilla must have been a capable worker in her own right for Paul to mention her along with her husband. I wasn't aware of any other co-worker of Paul ever having his wife's name mentioned together with him.

More than that, Paul usually placed Priscilla's name ahead of Aquila's. Did this remarkable woman excel her husband? Was she more outgoing than her mate, the better educated, the more Scripturally informed, the more profound teacher, the stronger character, the more articulate, the earlier and more mature Christian? She must have been an exceptional woman with outstanding gifts to qualify as teacher of someone so eloquent, so theologically competent, and so potentially useful as Apollos. She was an unusual woman, able to combine business matters, home duties, devotional life and Christian service.

Suggests Gilbert Bilezikian, "That a woman should have been permitted to play such a determinant role in the training of a key leader of the apostolic church has not always been easy to accept. In order to avoid divulging such a scandal, the translators of the King James version discreetly inverted the names of Priscilla and Aquila in Acts 18:26, thus preferring to commit violence on the text of Scripture rather than face the fact that God calls qualified women to be teachers" (*Beyond Sex Roles*, Grand Rapids: Baker Books, 1989, p. 202).

Priscilla and Aquila returned to Rome for several years. Paul, in Corinth toward the end of his third missionary journey, sent a letter to the church in Rome with this message: *Greet Priscilla and Aquila, my fellow workers in Christ Jesus. They risked their lives for me* (Romans 16:3-4, NIV). In no way did Paul consider her any less of a worker than her husband. Both were willing to die for him. Then Paul added, *Greet also the church that meets at their house* (vs. 5). Wherever they went, they had a church in their home, likely at Priscilla's initiative.

Priscilla has been suggested as a possible writer of the epistle to the Hebrews. This might help explain, some surmise, why the book was accepted as canonical but its authorship never mentioned.

THE CHURCH AT CAESAREA

On his way to Jerusalem toward the end of his travels, Paul and his group visited Philip the evangelist, who had settled down in Caesarea. Luke mentions that Philip *had four daughters, virgins, which did prophesy* (Acts 21:9). Whoever prophesied spoke to others to give edification, exhortation and comfort. If these daughters prophesied, they preached. I can't imagine that their messages were spoken in a vacuum, or in private, or just to their father. This gift would have been pointless unless exercised among the assembled church.

Not a single word gives the slightest hint of disapproval of the prophetic speaking of these four women. With the Holy Spirit's gift and approval, they had a ministry of prophecy. Paul mentions them, not because it was exceptional for a woman to prophesy, but because it was most unusual for four women in the same family to do so.

THE CHURCH AT CENCHREA

Paul gave this resounding endorsement of a woman from the church at Cenchrea (the eastern harbor of Corinth): *I commend unto you Phoebe our sister, which is a servant of the church which is at Cenchrea: That ye receive her in the Lord, as becometh saints, and that ye assist her in whatsoever business she hath need of you: for she hath been succourer of many, and of myself also* (Romans 16:1-2).

The translators of the King James Version show a masculine bias by making Phoebe sound like a lowly servant of the church, when, in keeping with the usual meaning of the word, Paul is really styling her as a deacon or minister. Only in reference to Phoebe does the King James Version translate *diakonos* as "servant." *Diakonos* occurs twenty-two times in the New Testament. Three times it is translated "deacon." Eighteen times it is translated "minister." For example, *Who then is Paul, and who is Apollos, but ministers by whom ye believed* (1 Corinthians 3:5). (Also 2 Corinthians 3:6; 6:4). If on every other occasion *diakonos* is translated either "deacon" or "minister," why is Phoebe called a "servant"? Was the idea of a woman minister intolerable to the King James translators?

I looked up some modern translators and found they did somewhat better. The Revised Standard Version and Phillips speak of her as a "deaconess," although the Greek has no feminine form, and thus no such word. The New International Version follows the King James Version, using "servant" with a footnote, "deaconess." But Living Letters is inconsistent. Whereas it calls the church leaders at Philippi and at Ephesus "deacons" (Philippians 1:1; 1 Timothy 3:8,12), it merely refers to Phoebe as "a dear Christian woman from the town of Cenchrea." Who could possibly tell from this version that Paul called her a deacon (or minister or servant)? Living Letters, whose paraphrases so often clarify the original, here clouds an important fact about a woman's role in ministry.

We do not know precisely what the duties of deaconesses were. Probably not church finances. More likely they visited the lonely, encouraged the downhearted, prayed with the sick and evangelized women, whose often isolated lives made them unreachable by male evangelists. The work Phoebe expended on the saints was far more than washing dishes, baking goods or running rummage sales. Despite the inconsistency and prejudice of translators, Phoebe was coming as the bearer of the epistle to the Romans, a treatise on the doctrine of salvation, perhaps the most important book Paul wrote. She was representing the church at Cenchrea, apparently with official business to conduct for which Paul, often the recipient of her staunch support, now asked their assistance. Paul could not have requested any more for the most devoted of male ministers than he asked for Phoebe: they were to give her whatever she needed. I could see that she held no trifling position in the early church.

THE CHURCH AT ROME

Nothing is known of the founding of the church at Rome, and very little is known of its activity, but the list of greetings in the last chapter of Paul's letter to that church gives some insight as to the composition of its membership. Of the twenty-seven persons mentioned by name in the first half, approximately one-third are women — a startlingly high proportion. The opening sequence (Romans 16:1-8) displays a balance: two women (Phoebe, Priscilla); two men (Aquila, Epaenetus); one woman (Mary), one man (Andronicus); one woman (Junia), one man (Amplias).

Some think Junia a man, but her name was a

common Greco-Roman feminine name. Church fathers like Chrysostom and Jerome refer to this person as a woman. When she is described as *of note among the apostles* (vs. 7), some take it to mean that she was numbered among some select list of apostles. More likely it means that she was outstanding in the opinion of the apostles. However, I didn't rule out the possibility of some distinctive service meriting the tag "apostle."

It is said of Mary (vs. 6), Tryphena, Tryphosa and Persis (vs. 12) that they worked hard for the Lord. This expression, which generally refers to participation in the work of the gospel, was here applied to women no differently than to men. I concluded that these ladies were more than maids-in-waiting, but rather like partners in church life, and even leadership.

THE CHURCH OF THE ELECT LADY

The Apostle John apparently wrote his second epistle *unto the elect lady and her children* (2 John 1). Some believe the lady represents the church, but this is hard to reconcile with the alternation between singular pronouns and plural forms throughout the letter. It's likely that "her children" refer to the congregation which met in her home, of which she may well have been the leader. The address to the elect lady parallels the address in John's third epistle *unto the well-beloved Gaius* (3 John 1). Gaius was undoubtedly a leader in his church; why not the elect lady in hers?

IMPRESSIONS

What impressions did I gain from gleaning the history of the New Testament church? Basically that, though the leaders were usually men, in some cases women played an important role in ministry. A bigger part may have been played by women in the Greek and Roman world than in the Jerusalem church, because greater freedom was enjoyed by women in those places. Paul seemed to grant more liberty where elevation of womanhood did not produce scandal. This equality had not been known in Judean religious practice. I discovered that Jesus' open attitude toward women carried over into the early church. Women had a new role in the church, not just as mothers, daughters, wives and table-servers, but as possessors of status, gifts and ministries.

A seminary class was studying the text from Isaiah which Jesus read in the synagogue at Nazareth: *"The Spirit of the Lord is on me, because He has anointed me to preach good news to the poor. He has sent me to proclaim freedom for the prisoners and recovery of sight for the blind, to release the oppressed, to proclaim the year of the Lord's favor"* (Luke 4:18-19, NIV).

The class was asked, "What role in the passage do you identify with?" Many of the men replied, "The preacher," the one proclaiming the good news. But not so for the women. Most of them sympathized with the poor, the prisoners, the blind and the oppressed — the recipients of the good news.

The model of the early church teaches that both men and women are called to be Spirit-controlled heralds and sympathizers with the downtrodden.

I wondered: Did women continue to play a part in ministry down through the centuries, or were they stifled and silent? So, I decided to look next into the place women played in church history.

5

Women In History

★ ★ ★

That Sunday in 1990 when Janna and I both preached in the same town in different churches at the same hour, my wife and I were guests in her home in Clinton, New York. We had arrived on Saturday, spent a lovely evening with Janna, husband Gene, and son Jeremy. On Sunday night, I began to feel dizzy, later waking up to find the wallpaper and furniture going in all directions. I could barely stand up, much less move across the room amidst the swirling, twirling walls, floor and ceiling.

The next morning, the first Monday in June, Janna decided to act. She was just finishing up, as part of her seminary training, a month-long internship in pastoral care at St. Elizabeth Hospital in Utica, about ten miles away, where each weekday from early morning until late afternoon she visited patients, counseling and comforting. Known and respected by the staff, she arranged for me to be admitted to the emergency room where I was diagnosed as having infections in both ears and given prescriptions by a nearby ear specialist. I spent the next four days at my daughter's, trying to regain my balance. Back home my doctor suggested I see a neurologist who recommended an MRI. When the picture showed mainly inflammation of the ears, the neurologist advised me to cancel my schedule of fifty speaking engagements for July and August. (When a speaker finds that he's swaying his audience before he begins to speak, he knows he's in trouble. It's tough when the wave comes to church.)

How strange it seemed to have the summer free from speaking responsibilities. That summer of 1990 was the first summer in thirty years that I had not spoken at two or three Bible conferences and supplied the pulpit in various churches. But my daughter, who for the first four decades of her life had not preached summer nor winter, was now scheduled to preach in various churches almost every summer Sunday. I went from fifty engagements to none; she from none to several. This episode kept me thinking about the role of women in ministry. How long had women been preaching, anyway?

EARLY CHURCH

In the ancient Roman catacomb of the two martyrs, Marcellino and Pietro, is a drawing of a woman raising the communion cup, with all eyes around the table fixed on her. Similar representations of women leaders, dating back to the first three centuries, are found on frescoes, carvings, tombs and mosaics. A picture of the above-mentioned drawing appeared in the National Association of Evangelical's publication, *Action*, (January-February, 1984, p. 9).

In the accompanying article, "Leaders Past and Present," author Catherine Kroeger, at that time a doctoral candidate in classical studies at the University of Minnesota, commented, "These early Christian women were committed to carrying on a ministry begun by their sisters in the faith who walked with Jesus and witnessed His death and resurrection." Susanne Heine, professor of theology at the University of Vienna, contends that they "traveled as missionaries and did charitable work; they preached, taught, gathered the believers together and sewed clothes for women" (*Women and Early Christianity: A Reappraisal*, trans. J. Bowden, Minneapolis: Augsburg Fortress, 1988, p. 90). She claims that the way they fulfilled their Christian vocation varied little from that of their male colleagues, but as the church accommodated itself to the surrounding patriarchal culture, it began to relegate women to subordinate positions.

THE WESLEYS

Historians have suggested that the modern emancipation of womanhood began with John Wesley. If so, some credit must be given to his mother,

Susanna. When her minister husband, Samuel, was absent for a prolonged period, Susanna, seeing the evening attendance dwindling because of poor preaching, started holding evening services in her kitchen. With the evening crowd soon outnumbering the morning flock and overflowing, the envious interim minister complained to Samuel in London, asking him to take immediate steps to stop this scandal. Susanna defended herself by writing that no man in the congregation had as strong a voice as hers, and that no one else could read well enough to lead the congregation in the liturgy.

When Samuel wrote, ordering her to stop, she claimed that the Lord had led her into this ministry, and recounted all the good being accomplished. But she did say that she would yield to him if he definitely put his foot down, thus absolving herself from all guilt and punishment for neglecting this opportunity of ministering God's Word. Knowing the problem would go away as soon as he returned home, Samuel did nothing. Thus, "Susanna Wesley won the first battle for women's lib as a true minister of the Gospel of Christ" (W.H. Daniels in *History of Methodism*, related in *Christian Heritage*, "The Methodist Women's Lib — 1689," January 1975, p. 20).

So we can't be surprised when John Wesley, with such a mother, in 1739 appointed women as class leaders in his new movement. The same patterns which encouraged the lay people in church leadership opened the way for women. When Wesley found that God used women, he said, "Who am I that I should withstand God?" The new role that was granted to women in the Evangelical Revival slowly enlarged to include preaching. In 1787, Wesley gave the right hand of fellowship to Sarah Mallete as a preacher so long as she adhered to Methodist doctrine and discipline.

INFLUENCE OF CHARLES G. FINNEY

Though Free Will Baptists allowed women to serve as preachers and itinerant evangelists before 1800, it was in the wake of the Second Great Awakening, and especially the revivalism of evangelist Charles G. Finney, that such practices developed into full ordination. One of his contested new ideas was permitting women to speak and pray in mixed congregations. As the president of Oberlin College, the first co-educational college in the world, Finney perpetuated his kind of revivalism and reform.

The anti-slavery movement and the women's rights movement, closely connected at this period, were both firmly rooted in Finney's revivalism. Those who defended slavery pointed to biblical examples of slavery and Paul's commands to slaves to be subservient. In answer, abolitionists affirmed that the apostles, while yielding temporarily to the institution of slavery, laid down principles which ultimately undercut the foundations of that horrible system. By adopting the same hermeneutical principle to the case against feminine subordination in ministry, the door was opened for women's role in ministry, even ordination. The first woman to be ordained in the Congregational Church was Antoinette Brown, who had graduated from Oberlin where she had insisted on sitting through the theological courses, usually open only to men.

Says Catherine Kroeger, "Ann Judson became the first of many thousands of American women missionaries. With growing involvement in outreach, women soon became key organizers of mission societies, Sunday schools, temperance and abolition societies. In the 1800's came Phoebe Palmer, an associate evangelist with D.L. Moody. Winning 25,000 on two continents to Christ, her preaching served as the impetus for the public ministries of Catherine Booth, co-founder of the Salvation Army, and of Francis Willard, founder of the Women's Christian Temperance Union and also an associate evangelist with Moody" (*Action*, January-February 1984, p. 9).

D.L. Moody's wife, Emma, shunned the spotlight but exercised her teaching gift in Moody's early days of Sunday School work as teacher of a class of forty middle-aged men. A visitor in the Sunday School, hinting at the impropriety of the situation, remarked, "Isn't that lady too young to be the teacher of a class of men like that?" Moody said he thought the teacher handled the class quite well. When the visitor kept complaining, Moody proudly said, "That, sir, is my wife."

CATHERINE BOOTH (1829-1890)

Born in Derbyshire, England, Catherine Booth had learned to read by age three, and by age twelve had read the Bible through eight times and was writing letters to temperance journals under a pen name. Though having little formal education, she read voluminously, including church history and theology. Converted at sixteen, she joined the Wesleyan Church. One Sunday night, when she was twenty-two, she was impressed with a sermon by an itinerant evangelist named William Booth. Soon they were corresponding. She told him of her conviction of a woman's right to preach.

Busy with three children in their first four and a half years of marriage, she was always sending William summaries, illustrations, articles and ideas of her own for his sermons. In 1859, upset by a neighboring minister's pamphlet attacking the right of women to preach, she wrote, with her husband's blessing, a strong rebuttal titled, *Female Ministry — Woman's Right to Preach the Gospel*, still published by the Salvation Army today. She pointed out that women in the early church prayed and prophesied publicly and that this was predicted for this age. She quoted Greek scholars, and noted biblical and historical examples of women used in the Lord's service. With strong logic she concluded, "If the Word of God forbids female ministry, we would ask how it happens that so many of the most devoted handmaidens of the Lord have felt themselves constrained by the Holy Ghost to exercise it. Surely there must be some mistake somewhere, for the Word and the Spirit cannot contradict each other. Either the Word does not condemn women preaching, or else those confessedly holy women have been deceived" (p. 17-18).

One Sunday morning when her husband called for testimonies, Catherine walked forward and confessed that, though a pastor's wife, she had been unfaithful to the gifts God had given her by not having a more public ministry. William, who for years had urged her to address congregations, immediately invited her to preach that evening. Soon after her pulpit debut, when her husband suffered a complete breakdown in health, she took over the entire preaching and pastoral ministry of his circuit. Not long later, feeling confined in their denominational connection, they resigned and branched out in a ministry to the masses of urban down-and-outers. Thousands came to her revival crusades, often advertised by the slogan, "Come and Hear a Woman Preach." Though bearing eight children, she juggled motherly and ministerial duties well. All became active in the ministry. One of her daughters started preaching at fourteen, winning thousands in France and Switzerland. The Salvation Army has ordained women from the very beginning. General Booth used to say, "Our best men are women."

MODERN MISSIONARY MOVEMENT

The achievements of women during nearly two centuries of the modern missionary movement are unparalleled in the history of Christianity. At no other period did women have so much latitude in Christian service. But not because church leaders had revised their theological convictions on women preachers, but mainly because not enough men volunteered for overseas duty. So women filled the ranks. During the period of 1900-1910, women outnumbered men in Protestant missions for the first time in history, often by as much as two to one. Although the surge of women into the ranks of missionaries during the last part of the nineteenth century may have been a reflection of the feminist movement in North America, the most obvious reason was the scarcity of opportunities for women to get involved in a full-time ministry in their homeland. Christian service was deemed a male profession. So missions, far from the church at home, became an outlet for women with a drive (and a call) to serve.

Women often took the hardest and most hazardous assignments. Virtually no part of the world went untouched by these vigorous female pioneers. Worldwide Evangelization Crusade had for one of its mottos, "The woman is the best man to do it." Another saying went, "The best man for a job is often a woman." Ironically, women often received little mention in the historical annals. Even when women manned the outposts in pioneering missionary organizations, they were soon replaced by men in leadership posts, and their freedom diminished as the hierarchical framework increased. To put it more bluntly, the women did the tough work, then the men came in and took over.

When home on furlough, these valiant crusaders of the cross are often considered second-class servants, unworthy of filling the pulpit on a Sunday morning. Even when they do, their ministry is couched in guarded terminology. Said one female missionary, "I have been allowed to preach in churches as long as I was not said to preach but to give an address or make a report." Another missionary accepted her first Sunday service back from overseas assignment on the pastor's stipulation that she answer questions from down at the front pew rather than up at the pulpit. Another missionary was asked to speak from behind a screen.

I recall on a trip to Africa in 1986, I was relaxing in Kigali, capital of Rwanda, by reading *From Jerusalem to Irian Jaya,* by Ruth A. Tucker (Grand Rapids: Zondervan, 1983). A chapter called, "Single Women Missionaries" (pp. 231-260) relates the remarkable labors of six women, Charlotte (Lottie) Diggs Moon, Amy Carmichael, Maude Cary, Johanna Veenstra, Helen Roseveare and Gladys Aylward, in mission work. Gladys Alyward's popular biography, *The Small Woman,* and film, *The Inn of Six Happinesses*, made her an international celebrity.,

She once confided to a friend, "I wasn't God's first choice for what I've done in China. There was somebody else.... It must have been a man — a wonderful man. A well-educated man. I don't know what happened. Perhaps he wasn't willing... and God looked down... and saw Gladys Aylward" (p. 254).

HENRIETTA MEARS (1890-1963)

Henrietta Mear's three decades of ministry as Director of Christian Education at the Presbyterian Church of Hollywood, California, has been called the most significant work among our nation's youth done by a woman in the twentieth century. The book, *Henrietta Mears and How She Did It* by Ethel May Baldwin and David V. Benson (Ventura: Regal Books, 1966), chronicles her accomplishments. Among them was the building of the largest Presbyterian Sunday School in the world, guiding it from four hundred and fifty to six thousand members. She wrote and published her own lesson curricula, resulting in the founding of Gospel Light Publications. She pioneered Forest Home, one of the country's most popular conference centers. She taught a class of about three hundred students in the college department on Sunday mornings.

When Dr. Clarence Roddy, homiletics professor at Fuller Seminary, was once asked who in his opinion was the best preacher in southern California, he immediately answered, "Henrietta Mears" (p. 121). But Mears did not like to be regarded as a preacher or pastor, for she thought these roles were for men. She preferred the title, "The Teacher," which became the name by which thousands of college students called her. She could teach the Bible to three hundred university students, male and female, in Sunday School, but did not feel she had the right to preach at the 11 a.m. hour to the entire congregation.

Her biographer said, "To challenge young men to enter the ministry was perhaps the greatest of Miss Mear's gifts. In the course of her career in Hollywood over four hundred collegians heard God's call and turned their energies to pulpits in America or to missionary stations scattered around the world" (p. 143). Among them were Richard Halverson, who became Chaplain of the US Senate, Bill Bright, founder of Campus Crusade, and Louis Evans, Jr., well-known Presbyterian pastor. She always purchased her budding ministers their "preacher's suit" and winter overcoat, if needed, to assure a well-groomed appearance in a dark suit whether preaching from a pulpit or officiating at a wedding.

It is rather ironic that she could influence hundreds of young men to enter a profession that was denied her, and could provide them with a ministerial suit when she herself could never wear the clergy collar.

CORRIE TEN BOOM

Corrie ten Boom lived a quiet life in Holland until the outbreak of World War II when she was in her fifties. Because she made her home a hiding place for Jews trying to escape Nazi terror, she was shipped to a concentration camp. Her brave story of divine protection midst Nazi atrocities and of her providential release projected her into a speaking and writing ministry that spanned more than sixty countries and three decades.

I shall never forget the Sunday evening Corrie ten Boom spoke at the church I pastored in Nanuet, New York. Over a thousand people crowded our facilities. How stirringly she preached the Word that night. But she wasn't always welcomed by churches. One letter of invitation read, "You understand that you may not teach us. You can give your testimony, but be Scriptural and obey 1 Corinthians 14:34,35." She replied, "If by this you mean that I must come with a closed Bible, then I cannot accept your invitation. I am always happy to give my testimony to glorify the Word of God, not to talk about my own experiences." Immediately came the answer, "Forget what we have written. We have heard that God is blessing your meetings." Corrie ten Boom spoke at the meeting.

We have discussed only a fraction of the women who have been involved in ministry. So many have been omitted: Hannah Whitall Smith who wrote one of the top best-sellers of the last 150 years, *The Christian's Secret of a Happy Life*, and who was an invited speaker at many of England's Bible Conferences; Mrs. Jessie Penn-Lewis (1861-1927), well-known in England as a Bible teacher, who also travelled in Canada, India, Russia and Scandinavia, as well as the USA evangelical circuit; Christabel Pankhurst of England who began her public ministry in 1921 and gained renown in America, travelling nationwide to speak at Bible conferences, often at Chicago's Moody Bible Institute and New York City's Calvary Baptist Church. Thousands professed conversion during her two decades of preaching.

To move to the present, how often at main sessions of national conventions have I been blessed by speakers such as Jill Briscoe, Elizabeth Elliott, Karen Mains and Rebecca Pippert.

FUNDAMENTALISM AT THE TURN OF THIS CENTURY

I was surprised to learn that many fundamentalist leaders around the turn of the century approved of women preachers. Raised in a tradition of disfavor toward women preachers, I had taken it for granted that fundamentalists had always held a negative view. In my research, I came across the book, *No Time For Silence* (Janette Hassey, Grand Rapids: Zondervan, 1985), which documents the acceptance by many fundamentalists of both the inerrancy of Scripture and the right of women to preach. Some of the following facts I culled from this book.

Dr. A.B. Simpson

North America's first Bible Institute, called the Missionary College for Home and Foreign Missions (now Nyack College) was started in New York City in 1881 by Dr. A.B. Simpson, founder of the Christian and Missionary Alliance. Simpson gave women a prominent place in virtually every phase of C&MA

life. A host of women served effectively as evange-lists, Bible teachers, professors, local ministers, and on executive boards. In 1887, half of all C&MA vice-presidents were women. At the 1888 graduation, the Nyack Institute awarded the preaching prize (for excellence in "Homiletic Exercises") to a woman. With his emphasis on missions, Simpson happily found that women proved as capable as men in car-rying the gospel to primitive tribes.

Dr. A.J. Gordon

Dr. A.J. Gordon, pastor of the Clarendon Street Baptist Church in Boston for twenty-four years, wrote a book, *The Ministry of Women,* in which he argued strongly for women's role in church life. With the encouragement of D.L. Moody, he started Boston Missionary Training School (now Gordon-Conwell Seminary) in 1889, open to women as well as men. Yearbooks indicate the wide influence of women graduates serving as pastors, missionaries, Bible teachers and preachers. A pastor-friend of mine told me that both of his parents attended Gordon's school and that at one time their professor of homiletics was a woman.

Gordon wrote in *The Alliance Weekly* (December 15, 1928), "It cannot be denied that in every great spiritual awakening in the history of Protestantism the impulse for Christian women to pray and witness for Christ in the public assembly has been found irrepressible.... Observing also the great blessing which has attended the ministry of consecrated women in heralding the Gospel, many thoughtful men have been led to examine the Word of God anew, to learn if it be really so that the Scriptures silence the testimony which the Spirit so signally blesses. To many it has been both a relief and a surprise to discover how little authority there is in the Word for repressing the witness of women in the public assembly, or for forbidding her to herald the Gospel to the unsaved. If this be so, it may be well for the plaintiffs in this case to beware lest in silencing the voice of consecrated women, they may be resisting the Holy Ghost. The conjunction of these two admonitions of the apostle is significant: *Quench not the Spirit. Despise not prophesyings* (1 Thessalonians 5:19-20)."

Dr. William B. Riley

Two years after Gordon's death, Dr. W.B. Riley began his forty-five year pastorate of Minneapolis' First Baptist Church. The leading fundamentalist of his day, he founded the World's Christian Fundamentals Association in 1919. To counteract the growing modernism in eastern seminaries, he founded Northwestern Bible and Missionary Training School in 1902.

A clue to his view on women's public ministry may be found in a sermon in 1901, where he says, "I recall the first time I ever heard Frances Willard speak. She was in a small southern city, where it was regarded a shame for a woman to appear on the platform with men in the assembly. But I confess, that I went from that house convinced that so long as saloons remained to embrute women's husbands, blight women's beautiful boys, blast women's lives... that every speech against it would be justified, no matter who made up the assemblies, and would be approved and applauded by that heavenly assembly of saints and angels... when in defense of all that is true, a suffering woman feels compelled to break the silence and speak against sin."

Under Riley's regime, Northwestern employed women preachers in its Extension Department, advertising, for example, the ministry of Miss Playfair open "to address Sunday or weekday meetings, church audiences... religious conferences or community gatherings of any kind." Several alumnae took pastorates in rural upper midwest communities, while others preached and evangelized with official school sanction.

MOODY BIBLE INSTITUTE

Mention has already been made of D.L. Moody's use of women as associate evangelists. His association with Emma Dryer, whom he referred to as "one of the best teachers of the Word of God in the United States," helped lead to the founding of Moody Bible Institute (Eric Fellman, "Emma Dryer: Visionary of a Bible School," *Moody Monthly*, May 1985, p. 84). In 1897, the Institute established an Extension

Department to promote school interests by organizing Bible conferences, supplying evangelists for revival meetings and providing churches with guest preachers. By 1928, the department had reached nearly a quarter of a million people through twenty-five MBI-sponsored conferences throughout the country. Several women were employed as evangelists and teachers. The August 1916 issue of *The Christian Workers Magazine* (now *Moody Monthly*) listed the names of three women as "our field Bible Teachers and Evangelists." As a student at Moody in 1937 (where I received training that I would not trade), one of my teachers was a woman — Frances C. Allison — who had previously served as a Bible teacher for Moody's Extension Department. When Catherine Booth made her headquarters at MBI for two months and preached twice at the famed Moody Church, MBI advertised that its Extension Department would receive inquiries for her services as an evangelist.

Trained with the skills for public ministry, *alumnae* served in pastorates in many denominations, mainly in small towns and rural areas of the midwest, and also in the evangelistic field. Scores of references to women preachers, pastors and evangelists, trained at MBI, were publicized in the Alumni News section of old *Moody Monthly* magazines. Though MBI didn't overtly encourage women to preach, its editorial policy seemed implicit endorsement of women in such ministry.

Though Moody Bible Institute does not today endorse or encourage the ordination of women,

President Joseph Stowell III said in *Moody Alumni* magazine (Spring 1991, p. 2), "Quite frankly, our forefathers were more tolerant in terms of women in ministry than some of us tend to be today."

JOHN ROACH STRATON

Founder of the Fundamentalist League of Greater New York and Vicinity and editor of the *Fundamentalist* magazine, John Roach Straton invited Uldine Utley, a woman evangelist and Bible teacher, to conduct a five-week revival in his pulpit at Calvary Baptist Church, New York City, in 1926.

Strongly criticized, Straton wrote a pamphlet, *Does the Bible Forbid Women to Preach and Pray in Public?*, in defense of his action. He also urged support for Utley's upcoming crusade at Calvary. His plea proved successful, for her meetings closed with 10,000 people at a rally in Madison Square Garden.

DR. L.E. MAXWELL

Dr. L.E. Maxwell, president of Prairie Bible Institute which he founded in 1922, authored a posthumously published book, *Women in Ministry* (Wheaton: Victor Books, 1987). The manuscript was carefully prepared from his notes by Ruth Dearing, who worked closely with him during her long association with the school. This woman had served on the Board of Directors, was Principal of the High School for eighteen years and taught Bible in the college for many years. She was able to complete and receive his endorsement on two-thirds of the manuscript before his death. She finished the book, presenting the material as closely as possible to the way Maxwell had prepared it. Dearing wrote in the introduction, "The work represents the cream of his study and thinking over a considerable period of time.... Since Mr. Maxwell often talked with me about his concern for women in Christian ministry and at various times had read to me what he and others had written, I believe I understand his thinking about the whole issue and trust I have communicated this in the finished product" (p. 12).

According to Dearing, Maxwell's conviction was that women should not be barred from public ministry, though he never went so far as to make a case for their ordination. "His desire was that women might be set free from what he felt were unscriptural restrictions placed on them by many churches and Christian leaders" (p. 11). He purposed in this book to justify women's privilege and liberty to participate in public ministry. The school he founded was engaged in the training of women as well as men for public ministry (p. 13).

INDEPENDENT FUNDAMENTAL CHURCHES OF AMERICA

In 1923, midwest ministers who contested liberalism and denominationalism formed the American Conference of Undenominational Churches (ACUC).

Women who met the criteria were received into full membership. This openness was seen in the use of "his" and "her" in the constitution. When the ACUC changed its name to the Independent Fundamental Churches of America (IFCA) in 1930, its constitution eliminated women from membership. At the time, thirteen of its one hundred and seventy-four members were women, ordained and serving as pastors or assistant pastors.

DR. HENRY SAVAGE

Dr. Henry Savage, a long-time pastor of the First Baptist Church of Pontiac, Michigan, the leading fundamentalist in his state and a nationally-known Bible teacher, firmly defended the right of Amy Stockton, a member of his church, to serve as an evangelist. Savage always included her as one of the main speakers at Maranatha Bible Conferences which featured the outstanding fundamentalist speakers that traveled the summer conference circuit. Stockton held evangelistic campaigns all over the United States. Dr. Clarence Sands, an esteemed Baptist pastor, was converted during one of her crusades. Another of her converts, Dr. Timothy Slater, had an illustrious career as a medical missionary in Africa.

Other Christian leaders owe their conversion to women preachers. For example, Larry McGuill, the well-known evangelist and church planter, made his decision for Christ in a 1914 crusade in Ridgewood, New Jersey, led by Irene Brainerd, who spent twenty years in evangelism after her graduation from Practical Training School in Binghamton, New York.

THE PROBLEM

Summing up: Many evangelical Bible institutes in their early years furnished women with the training to be preachers, pastors, and Bible teachers. These schools often publicized the pastoral placement and experiences of feminine graduates. Also, the institutes hired female evangelists and Bible teachers for outreach through their Extension Departments. Many early summer Bible conferences featured woman Bible teachers. Several leading fundamentalist pastors welcomed women preachers to their pulpits.

However, between World Wars I and II, fundamentalists began to bar women from their pulpits. The question is: Why the change? If the turn-of-the-century fundamentalists approved of women preachers, why did later fundamentalists oppose women's public ministry? Obviously, one's belief in biblical inerrancy was not the decisive reason. Those who held to biblical authority stood on both sides of the issue.

Hence, the problem: Why the shift from FOR to AGAINST? I would need to solve the paradox of "fundamentalist feminism."

6

Women:
Property or Partners

★ ★ ★

In the summer of 1990, just before the start of her third and final year of seminary, Janna received a letter from the Paris Hill United Church of Christ, inviting her to become its interim pastor. It would just be for a short period until a larger church, with whom they shared a pastor, could call a new minister. Only six miles from her home, Janna had filled the pulpit on several occasions. Since attendance averaged about thirty out of a membership of one hundred, Janna knew that her responsibilities would not be too taxing on her academic load. She learned that the trustees had not had a meeting for ten years. The church had no news letter, but agreed to publish one to inform the congregation of the new time of service. Janna planned to visit all the members. She accepted the call to begin on September 1.

Denominational policy required ministerial candidates to appear before the area association "Church and Ministry Committee" at the time of their decision to go to seminary and every year thereafter until ordination. At her annual appearance in August, Janna was temporarily licensed to conduct weddings and funerals. She served the church until the end of September, when a new pastor took over. Though she served only a month, I said to myself, "I already have a daughter who has actually been a pastor, even if only for a short interim. It's all the more imperative that I get on with my study of the role of women. Many loose threads still remain that need clearing up." One of these threads was the question of equality. Are men to have authority over women? Or are they to consider them equal? Are women servants or partners? Is the relationship hierarchical or egalitarian? Where would my study lead me? Here are some truths I reviewed.

BOTH MEN AND WOMEN WERE CREATED IN THE IMAGE OF GOD

On the sixth day of creation, *God said, "Let us make man in our image, after our likeness...." So God created man in His own image, in the image of God created He him; male and female created He them* (Genesis 1:26-27).

Nothing in this account indicates that man is superior, or that woman is inferior. It does not suggest any difference in rank. Both man and woman bear the image of God. Woman shares with man all the privileges of personhood. Though differences exist, the great equalizer is their creation in the image of God. As people, they are co-equal.

God is neither male nor female. His essence includes not only so-called masculine characteristics, but feminine traits as well. For example, the heavenly Father pities His children. His children are also as those whom a mother comforts. It requires both male and female to fully reflect facets of the Creator's nature.

Absent from the creation account in both Genesis 1 and 2 is any command for man to exert authority over woman. Woman, like man, was created a little lower than the angels, but not lower than man. Man was not given dominion over woman. Rather, both man and woman were jointly given command over nature.

BOTH WERE GIVEN DOMINION OVER NATURE

After God created male and female, He ordered them, *"Be fruitful, and multiply, and replenish the earth, and subdue it: and have dominion over the fish of the sea, and over the fowl of the air, and over every living thing that moveth upon the earth."* (Genesis 1:28). Both man and woman were told to subdue the earth and exercise dominion over all other living things. This series of commands is often termed the cultural mandate, calling for a wise, non-wasteful, non-polluting use of the environment. This mandate also makes man and woman responsible for developing the many possibilities resident in creation, including participation in all spheres of human activity such as science, art, philosophy and politics. I recalled reading of a woman who asked herself, "Would God create me with a desire for the full development of my potential as a human being, and then set up a relationship that would thwart the fulfillment of those yearnings?"

The creation story contains two references to authority involving humans. First, God commands Adam to cultivate the garden, but prohibits him from eating of the tree of the knowledge of good and evil. This first line of authority is the sovereignty of God over mankind. The second line of authority is for man and woman to have dominion over the earth and its animal creatures. So the hierarchical structure at creation is God over man, and man and woman jointly over nature.

I noted the absence of any heavenly dictum that tells man to exercise authority over woman. If God designed man to rule over woman, surely He would have clearly included the order along with the other two hierarchical commands. The omission of authority ranking between man and woman shows that while God is over Adam and Eve, and Adam and Eve are over nature, neither Adam nor Eve has the right to boss the other.

Arguments from Genesis 2
Suggesting the Subordination of Woman

I found four main arguments repeatedly surfacing from Genesis 2 to show a supposed superiority of man over woman, making her part of the creation under his domination.

1. Woman was created after man.
2. Woman was taken out of man.
3. Woman was named by man.
4. Woman was created to be man's helper, thus subordinate.

Sometimes termed the "second creation story," Genesis 2 is an amplification of God's final creative act, the forming of man and woman. It is a close-up, a slow-motion replay of the sixth day, showing details that, to some, reveal woman to be secondary to man. But I asked myself, "Do these arguments hold up?"

1. The argument that Adam was superior to Eve because she came later seems to boomerang. If what comes later in the order of creation is inferior, then Adam is inferior to the animals, and the animals inferior to plant life. In reality, the order in Genesis 1 proceeds day by day from the inferior to the superior, so that man, the crown of creation, has dominion over the creations of the earlier days. On the same basis, since woman was created after man, should we not infer that woman is superior to man and should have domination over him? Would she not qualify as the supreme expression of God's creation?

2. That woman was taken out of man does not stress their difference, but rather their relatedness. Eve's origin from man's rib shows her superiority to the animals, not her inferiority to Adam. Woman being taken from man establishes the unity of the human race and the identical substance of man and woman, more so than if each had been a separate creation from dust. Adam responds to Eve as someone like himself, bone of his bone, and flesh of his flesh. Though Paul says, *For the man is not of the woman; but the woman of the man* (1 Corinthians 11:8), he adds, *For as the woman is of the man, even so is the man also by the woman* (vs. 12). Woman was created from man, but every man is born of woman, and that depicts the interweaving of equality.

How interesting, I thought, that in the mention of marriage (Genesis 2:24), the man, leaving home, is to cleave to his wife. "Cleave" is used almost universally as a weaker cleaving to a stronger, which, in this case, would suggest that man is the weaker.

3. In calling Eve "woman," Adam is not claiming authority over her, but recognizing and rejoicing in their mutuality. Though Adam does name her "Eve" after the fall (Genesis 3:20), I found it difficult to see how giving a person a name denotes headship over the recipient. When God summons the animals to Adam, it is to find a suitable helper, not to set up an operating chart with lines of authority.

4. It has been argued that because God made woman a helper to Adam, she is therefore subordinate to him, as a nurse to a doctor, a lab assistant to

a researcher, or a secretary to an executive. On this rationale, man is the boss, the woman his assistant. But of the approximately twenty times "helper" is used in the Old Testament, fifteen are used in reference to God as the helper of His people. In no way when we call God our helper are we making Him secondary to us. A person can only offer help from a position of strength. Thus the word "helper" may not be used to infer female subordination. The argument can be turned around to suggest her superiority. The word shows how helpless the man would have been in the Garden without her. He needed her to help accomplish their God-given mission, to walk beside him and to work with him, because she corresponded to him in every essential way.

BOTH SHARED IN THE FALL

Often the blame for the Fall is put on woman. True, Eve ate the forbidden fruit, making her guilty. But so did Adam, and with greater culpability. Unlike Eve, he had received the prohibition directly from God. Eve was deceived by the tempter, but when Adam willingly took of the fruit from her hand without raising any objection, he was not partaking of it blindly — he knew full well what he was doing. Though he blamed the woman for giving him the fruit, the Bible puts the fault for the Fall at the feet of Adam. God holds Adam responsible for dragging the race down. The Bible puts it, *By one man sin entered into the world, and death by sin* (Romans

5:12). The thesis that women are inferior to men because Eve brought sin into the world does not seem to hold.

One result of the Fall was male dominance. The Lord said to Eve, *Thy desire shall be to thy husband, and he shall rule over thee* (Genesis 3:16). He would now rule over her. Instead of a mate she finds a master. He lords it over her, puts her in her place, bullies her. Joint domination has become male domination, which does not seem to have been God's intent before the Fall. The rule of man over woman seems to be one result of the Fall.

BOTH SHARE IN REDEMPTION

Christ's intent, as part of His redemptive work, was to reverse the consequences of the Fall. If the Fall put woman down, salvation lifts her up. How revolutionary Jesus' teachings and actions toward women must have sounded to His hearers with their strongly negative attitude toward the distaff side. In those three years Jesus prepared His followers for the liberation proclamation of Pentecost which announced that women, as well as men, would prophesy. Women are joint heirs of God's grace. The redeemed community does not discriminate between slave and free, Jew and Gentile, nor does it perpetuate subordination of women to men. Paul's statement, *There is neither Jew nor Greek, there is neither bond nor free, there is neither male nor female: for ye are all one in Christ Jesus* (Galatians 3:28), has been called the Magna Carta of humanity. In Christ's Kingdom, all the benefits, responsibilities, and accountability belong to everybody, despite social station, race or sex.

All believers, women and men, receive the same forgiveness of sin, the same removal of guilt, the same gift of eternal life and the same seal of the Spirit. Women are baptized, join the church and take the Lord's Supper. Women worship with men, have common access to God, have their prayers answered, share in the indwelling presence of the Holy Spirit, in the priesthood of believers and in the assurance of heaven. In relation to God, men and women stand in precisely the same position. No wonder the spread of Christianity always elevates the status of women.

F.F. Bruce in a *Christianity Today* interview stated, "Personally, I could not countenance a position which makes a distinction of principle in church service between men and women. My own understanding of Christian priesthood is quite different from the understanding that dominates so much of the current discussion of the subject. If, as evangelical Christians generally believe, Christian priesthood is a privilege in which all believers share, there can be no reason that a Christian woman should not exercise her priesthood on the same terms as a Christian man" (April 7, 1989, pp. 24-25).

Many see a similarity between the abolition of slavery and the elevation of womanhood. Paul did not order slaves to rebel against their masters and demand their freedom. Paul did not command Philemon to emancipate his runaway slave, Onesimus, though he hinted at it rather strongly in his delicately composed epistle. New Testament remarks to slaves were aimed at comforting and teaching those caught in an institution which could not be changed overnight. But Christians, putting into practice the liberating principles of brotherhood, slowly, progressively and ultimately brought about the abolition of slavery. Similarly, statements about female submission were meant to comfort and instruct women in a situation which would slowly change as the principle of equality worked its way into church and society. Consistency seems to require that those who insist on keeping women in the subordinate role of the first century must also insist upon the reinstatement of slavery as found at that time.

Dr. Robert E. Speer, the top executive of the Presbyterian USA Board of Foreign Missions for forty-six years, argued for a a high view of women in Christian service. "It would be strange and anomalous to deny to women equality in the church, which is the very fountain of the principle of equality. It is Christ who has made woman free and equal. Is she to be allowed this freedom and equality elsewhere, and denied it in the Church, where freedom and equality had their origin? The Christian Churches on the foreign mission field are apprehending the measure of the Gospel in this better than we.... God shuts no door to His daughters which He opens to His sons" (W. Reginald Wheeler, *A Man Sent From God*, Grand Rapids: F.H. Revell Co., 1956, p. 163).

BOTH HELD POSITIONS OF LEADERSHIP IN THE OLD TESTAMENT

Scattered throughout the Old Testament are instances of women in authority. The history of Israel does not exhibit a uniform pattern of exclusive male leadership. Even if female leaders are the exception, the presence of even one woman exercising divinely bestowed authority shows that God intended some women to have leadership office.

Miriam

God classes Miriam with Moses and Aaron, her two brothers and both prophets, as having a part in Israel's deliverance from bondage. *For I brought thee up out of the land of Egypt, and redeemed thee out of the house of servants; and I sent before thee Moses, Aaron, and Miriam* (Micah 6:4). After this victory, Miriam, called "the prophetess," led the women in a great song of Moses, as one who had a part in Israel's triumph (Exodus 15:20). Miriam seems to be the first of a long series of godly women in Holy Writ who exercise a semi-ministerial service.

Deborah

After twenty years of oppression, God raised up *Deborah, a prophetess, the wife of Lapidoth,* to become a judge in Israel (Judges 4:4). With the authority of a prophetess, she revealed God's will to Israel. As a judge, she exercised judicial power,

103

rendering decisions which were submitted to in the same way the verdicts of the male judges who preceded and succeeded her were obeyed. When Barak, commander-in-chief of the Israelite army, was too fearful to go to war without her, she virtually became the military head, telling Barak what strategy to employ, resulting in the complete rout of the enemy. To add insult to injury, the fleeing enemy commander was killed by Jael, another woman. The exploits of both women are immortalized in a poem (Judges 5). The land had peace for forty years, mainly because of two women.

Huldah

Two spiritual ministries existed side by side in Israel: the priestly and the prophetic. Priests, who represented people to God, were limited to men of the Levitical tribe. All other men, as well as women, were barred from that office. The priesthood was entered exclusively by genealogy and gender, and not by divine call or spiritual giftedness. On the other hand, prophets spoke for God to the people, often correcting priestly misbehavior and denouncing royal wrongdoing. The prophetic ministry was not dependent on ancestry, but on call and enduement. Women, as well as men, were prophets, like Huldah.

When young king Josiah realized the precarious moral state of his nation through discovery of the lost book of the law, he sent several notables to the prophetess Huldah to seek the counsel of the Lord.

It was not because no male prophets were available that the king sought a woman. Jeremiah, Habakkuk and Zephaniah were all well-known contemporaries. Punctuating her answer with several "Thus saith the Lord's," Huldah's scathing denunciation of the nation's decadence, along with the prediction of doom, motivated the king to institute reform (2 Kings 22:11-23:25). Many men today reject, even despise, the teaching of a woman, but here a godly king of Judah had no trouble accepting a message delivered by a prophetess.

Two Old Testament books are named after women: Ruth and Esther. Some have wondered if the occasional breakthrough of Old Testament women VIP's may show God's displeasure at the suppression of women in Israel's culture. Also some suggest that God's granting of top spots in Israel to some women, limited as the number may be, foreshadows what He intended to do on a much grander scale in the church through the gospel.

BOTH ARE RECIPIENTS OF SPIRITUAL GIFTS

In the early 1970's, I preached a series of twenty-one sermons on spiritual gifts, which resulted in a book, *19 Gifts of the Spirit* (Wheaton: Victor Books, 1974). I well remember in a question-and-answer period someone asking, "Are there any gifts limited to men only?" I replied that I could find no place in Scripture which denied any gift to either sex. None of the major passages (Romans 12; Ephesians 4; 1 Corinthians 12) specify any gift as gender-directed. All gifts are bestowed on men and women alike. None is labeled, "For men only." Since the Lord wants His gifts to be discovered, developed and deployed in the church, does it not follow that men and women are equal in their employment of gifts in the service of the church? Men and women are equally redeemed, equally Spirit-filled, equally gifted, equally serving.

Often in churches, roles are tacitly and neatly categorized. Men are preachers, elders, trustees, board members and teachers of adult classes. Women change diapers, chase toddlers, bake pies, roll bandages, serve dinners and teach grade-schoolers. A woman with a theological bent, administrative gift, or preaching inclination, usually has to forget it. As Archie Bunker once advised an ambitious woman, "Stifle yourself! God don't want to be defended by no dingbat!"

In his first Corinthian epistle, Paul supports the right of women along with men to pray and prophesy in the public service. *Every man praying or prophesying, having his head covered, dishonoreth his head. But every woman that prayeth or prophesieth with her head uncovered dishonoreth her head* (1 Corinthians 11:4-5). How else should we understand Paul unless he is implying that women, as well as men, usually participate in public prayer and prophecy? It would be illogical for him to explain how to do something that was not permitted and customary.

Dr. Adam Clarke in his *Commentary on First Corinthians* says, "Whatever may be the meaning of praying and prophesying in respect to the man, they have precisely the same meaning in respect to the woman. So that some women, at least, as well as some men, might speak to others *to edification, and exhortation and comfort* (1 Corinthians 14:3,31). And this kind of prophesying or teaching was predicted by Joel 2:28, and referred to by Peter in Acts 2:17. And had there not been such gifts bestowed on women, the prophecy could not have had its fulfillment" (Nashville: Abingdon Cokesbury, n.d., p. 250).

BOTH WILL BE ACCOUNTABLE FOR THEIR GIFTS

Question 55 of the Heidelberg Confession reads, "What do you understand by the communion of saints?" The answer is, "First that believers, all and everyone, as members of Christ, are partakers of Him and of all His treasures and gifts; second, that everyone must know himself bound to employ his gifts readily and cheerfully for the advantage and salvation of other members."

All believers, including women, will be judged some day as to their faithfulness in employing their gifts. Leaders also will be judged as to whether they have encouraged Christian women in the Lord's service, or whether they have put road blocks in their way. Is the church making opportunity for Christian women to utilize their gifts? Stuart Briscoe wrote in

Moody Monthly, "I have a dread of burying someone else's talents, particularly those bestowed on women... a talent is a terrible thing to waste."

Dr. Earl Radmacher, for many years the president of Western Baptist Seminary, tells of receiving a letter from a woman with this question, "What will be my accountability at the judgment seat of Christ when I have to stand before Him and confess that I could not use my spiritual gift in my local church?" Radmacher commented that the woman's plea was pathetic, then added, "Oh God, the responsibility of leadership; to not just allow someone to use his or her gift but to see to it that every believer has a viable opportunity to use his or her gift in the local church." He pointed out that the woman was willing to obey the leadership of her church as exhorted in Hebrews 13:17 (Tape message, *Women in Ministry* at the Conservative Baptist Annual Meetings in Anaheim, CA, July 1990).

It seemed to me that women were equally created, equally redeemed, equally Spirit-controlled, equally gifted, equally sent, equally serving and equally accountable. But the nagging question kept lingering. Is the office of a pastor or elder Scripturally permissible to a woman? Though possessing all the gifts, are women limited in their teaching ministry to their own sex and to children? And are they denied the place of authority and leadership in church life? If women possess equality, what about 1 Corinthians 14:34 where women are told to keep silent in the churches?

And what about 1 Timothy 2:12 where women are told not to teach, nor to usurp authority over the man, but to be silent?

And what about Ephesians 5:22 where wives are told to *submit [them]selves unto [their] own husbands, as unto the Lord*? Is the husband the head of the house and boss over his wife? Or does equality extend to the marriage relationship?

7

Interpreting
An Inspired Bible

★ ★ ★

As Janna finished her second year of seminary, I learned to my surprise and delight that my own denomination would present at its annual meeting in the summer of 1990 a paper on the role of women in ministry. Shortly before the convention, a copy of this paper, the product of a two-year process, was sent to all pastors with the notation that no debate would be permitted until the following annual meeting in 1991. This moratorium was meant to provide an open climate for continuing study on "one of the most sensitive issues facing the Christian world today." I hoped the information in this study would help me in my personal pursuit, as I faced the prospect of having a daughter in the ministry. And it did.

Dr. Earl D. Radmacher who had selected the study committee of eight members from our denomination's seminaries, presented the paper. In the tape of his presentation he said that he was excited that our denomination had decided to tackle the problem. He moved through the paper in summary fashion, giving background material and synopses of the three main positions: egalitarian (evangelical feminist), moderate (centrist) and hierarchical (traditional).

In his introduction, he stressed the importance of distinguishing between inspiration and interpretation. Since our denomination unequivocally held to inerrancy, the question of woman's role was addressed from the basis of the authority of Scripture. "Sometimes," he said, "we treat our interpretation with the same mentality as we treat inspiration. We treat our interpretation as infallible and inerrant as we do the Scriptures themselves, and that is a sad mistake."

He cited the example of the Roman Catholic church which for years taught that the earth was the center of our solar system, even condemning Galileo as a heretic for asserting that the sun, not the earth, was the center. When scientific discoveries made it necessary for the church to re-examine its interpretation of Scripture, it concluded that the Scripture did not in any place explicitly teach that the earth was the center of the solar system. Calvin and Wesley, also, were both mistakenly taught, on the authority of the Word of God, that the earth was the center of the solar system. In this instance, the advance of science helped church leaders, both Catholic and Protestant, to rectify an earlier misinterpretation.

Radmacher emphasized the need to understand both the culture in which the books of the Bible were written, as well as today's culture. This may lead to a serious examination, not of our commitment to truth, but of our interpretation of it. Changing a cherished interpretation does not compromise our stand on inspiration, because it is the Word of God, not our interpretation, that is inerrant.

Sometimes, when traditional viewpoints are challenged, we tend to become emotional, instead of rational. Some of our ministers, discussing the study on woman's role a few weeks in advance of our annual 1990 meetings, heatedly remarked, "I haven't read the paper and I don't intend to. My mind is made up. If our denomination ever ordains women, I'm leaving." But as Radmacher commented, "Before we demonstrate heat, be sure to have light." We must not insert our emotions into our study of the Word just because we want our position to win. Nor should our cherished interpretations be held so dogmatically that, when others call them into question, we react as though they were doubting the inerrant Word of God. We should ever be striving to refine our fallible interpretations of the infallible Word. As Oswald Chambers warned, "It is a dangerous thing to refuse to go on knowing" (*Daily Thoughts for Disciples*, Grand Rapids: Zondervan, 1976, p. 215).

At this point I wondered if the verses, cited so frequently and emphatically to deny the right of women to speak in the church, could be put under the searchlight of further study. Do 1 Corinthians 11:34,

1 Timothy 2:11-12 and Ephesians 5:22 silence and subordinate women in the church, or do they have alternative interpretations?

1 CORINTHIANS 14:34-35

In these verses, Paul wrote, *Let your women keep silence in the churches: for it is not permitted unto them to speak; but they are commanded to be under obedience, as also saith the law. And if they will learn anything, let them ask their husbands at home: for it is a shame for women to speak in the church.*

At one period, because of this verse, church choirs were totally male, and boys whose voices had not yet changed were used to sing the soprano part. Sebastian Bach was once summoned before a local church council because, according to the official records, he had recently caused "the strange maiden to be invited into the choir loft and let her make music there." The strange maiden was his fiancee. Whether she posed as a boy soprano or simply sang while Bach practiced at the organ, it was a serious offense to allow a woman to sing in the choir loft.

If this verse is to be taken literally, it would seem that women today would not be permitted to sing solos in the church service, or even be in the choir. Nor could they give a testimony in the corporate gathering of the church, nor join in the singing of hymns nor in the unison reading of Scripture or creed, nor utter an audible amen, nor teach Sunday school, nor serve on our boards, nor offer opinions in our business sessions. Though most do not take so extreme a position, many on the basis of this passage object to women teachers or preachers.

Dr. W.H. Savage once said concerning the church, "Imagine three women meeting together in the name of the Lord Jesus Christ, longing to worship Him in song and testimony, but all three speechless, because a woman's voice must not be heard glorifying God!" Then he adds "Let's be consistent; either a woman's voice must not break the silence of any assembly, whether small or large; or, give her an opportunity, if the Spirit leads, to proclaim the gospel" (L.E. Maxwell with Ruth C. Dearing, *Women in Ministry*, Wheaton: Victor Books, 1987, p. 100).

But do these verses prohibit all speaking by women in the church? Many Bible scholars do not think so, especially since earlier in the same book Paul referred acceptably to women praying and prophesying in the church (1 Corinthians 11:5). The common-sense approach to this apparent discrepancy is that there is a proper kind of speaking for women, such as in the devotional and worship exercises of the church, and an improper type, as forbidden here.

What constitutes improper speaking? The word for "speak" in 1 Corinthians 14:34-35 means more than merely talking or saying. The various lexicons include the following meanings: to prattle, chatter, babble as a child, harangue, plead, make an inarticulate sound as opposed to intelligible speech. Paul is not demanding an absolute silence, but prohibiting an inappropriate kind of speaking. Apparently in some of the services at Corinth, women were interrupting, questioning, finding fault, disputing, making dogmatic assertions, even attempting to domineer. Such behavior was shameful. The word for "speak" is not the one that signifies purposeful, premeditative and prudent talk. Rather, it applies to speech that runs on. Paul's use of the present infinitive indicates continuous action, a tongue that keeps wagging away.

The women were interrupting the service by loudly asking questions. Since men were more educated, they listened attentively to the preaching. Not so with women whose lack of understanding led them to ask their husbands what the speaker meant. Their questioning, whether during the singing of a hymn or the teaching of the Word, produced a buzzing which disturbed the worship. Since neither heathen temples nor Jewish synagogues were models of reverence, Paul wanted to correct irregularities in the worship services of the new bands of believers, so rebuked this disorderly conduct of women. Significantly, Paul precedes his instruction by saying, *God is not the author of confusion, but of peace, as in all churches....* (vs. 33), and follows it with, *Let all things be done decently and in order* (vs. 40).

To correct disorder, Paul told the women not to become heady with self-assertion, but to practice self-control and wait and ask their husbands at home. Greek scholar Spiros Zodhiates says that Paul "does not speak about women in general, but about the wives of husbands who were with them in the assembly of believers worshiping Christ. Such husbands ought to take the responsibility of ensuring proper behavior by their wives" (*Women in the Home and Church*, Chattanooga: AMG Publishers, 1990, p. 15). He also believes the translation should not be, *Let your women*, but, *Let your wives be silent....* (vs. 34).

In reality, Paul was not dealing with whether or not women should preach, but with decorum in the church. It was not about women speaking in the pulpit, but about women interrupting in the pew. Instead of pandemonium and quarreling, he wished solemn worship with no disruptive deportment. In the enthusiasm of their new faith, some women took too much of a public role, speaking out far beyond the boundaries permitted by their culture, bringing disrepute on the church, and hindering the progress of the gospel. Some historians also suggest that newly converted Greek women who had indulged in orgiastic Orphic cultic ceremonies had imported noisy, ecstatic elements into the church service from their pre-Christian days. Such conduct Paul rebuked, favoring orderly, calm, rational worship.

1 TIMOTHY 2:8-15

When an association of Tennessee churches expelled a congregation from their fellowship in 1987, they cited this passage in 1 Timothy, probably the strongest and most quoted in favor of closing the mouths of women preachers. Many would say that these verses deny women the authoritative position of pastor or elder.

Some, on the basis of verses 8-10, claim that women should not pray in church. In reality, these verses approve and exhort an orderly participation of both men and woman in public prayer. In verse 8, men are told how to pray. Then verse 9 turns to women with a parallel command that they *in like manner* are to pray with modest apparel — no braids, no jewelry, no costly clothes. Paul had earlier told Corinthian women to pray with veiled heads. His instruction here harmonizes with the Corinthian advice.

Is this prohibition binding on women today? Most Bible scholars would say that the specific application by Paul had reference to first-century culture, and would not apply to Christian women of the twentieth century; women today do wear fancy hairdos, jewelry and fine clothes. The basic teaching here, and the principle normative for all generations and cultures, is that inner godliness is far more important than outer ornamentation.

A vital problem for the interpreter of Scripture is to decide what is cultural and what is transcultural. Immediately following the injunction on feminine attire comes a strong series of commands, beginning at verse 11: women are to learn in silence with all subjection; women are not to teach; women are not to usurp authority over men, but to be in silence. Now comes the question: Are these commands to be literally followed in all ages, or are they, like the immediately preceding dress code, culturally restricted?

Interestingly, many commentators believe this injunction is limited to the family, having nothing to do with sending women out to preach the gospel, but with the private home life and domestic character of a wife. No wife through her teaching or deportment should give the impression that she was putting a ring through her husband's nose and mastering him. One reason for thinking that the context is family life is the change from the plural "women" and "men" in verses 8-10 to "the woman" (vs. 11) and "the man" (vs. 12), both singular and possibly referring to wife and husband. Martin Luther's German version of verse 12 says, "I permit not a wife to teach nor have dominion over her husband." Another reason is that the verses following (vs. 13-14) refer to Adam and Eve, not just man and woman, but husband and wife. And verse 16 speaks of childbearing, a vital family function. No domineering posturing of a woman over her husband and a forcing of her theological opinions on him is worth the price of a wrecked marriage.

Certainly the apostle is not forbidding a woman to absolutely, unconditionally, completely and universally never teach. The most fanatic opponents of women preachers would allow a woman to teach her children, other women and even her own husband if he were ignorant of salvation and wanted to learn. Paul is not prohibiting teaching, but a certain kind of teaching, perhaps the type that would endanger marriage.

Several commentators explain that a decent Greek woman participating actively in a public meeting would brand her as an immoral woman, giving the church a bad reputation. Further, the situation at Ephesus (where Timothy was pastoring when Paul wrote him) required a caution about women teachers. Unlearned but pushy women had created considerable havoc because of their misguided enthusiasm. Paul warned of women going from door to door, peddling erroneous views (1 Timothy 5:13). Paul's solution was to forbid women who were still in the learning stage to become teachers.

The statement in verse 12, *I do not permit a woman to teach or to have authority over a man; she must be silent* (NIV), appears in English to be so absolute, final and universal. But in the original, according to Greek authorities, the word is gentler and more relative. The verb is not imperative, but indicative. Paul is not saying, "Don't you allow a woman to teach or have authority over a man." Rather, he is saying, "I, Paul, at this time, do not permit a woman to teach or to have authority over men. In this situation, under these particular circumstances, I do not allow a woman to teach." Paul's words were not a categorical command, but a description of how he was operating in that cultural context. The implication is that the condition could change. Later, when women there had grown in knowledge and grace after sitting humbly under the ministry of authorized teachers, nothing could prevent them from serving as teachers. Paul certainly permitted Priscilla to teach. His close workers in many places were women, like Euodias and Syntyche at Philippi. Likely Paul would have appreciated the ministry of Corrie ten Boom, had they lived in the same century.

Dr. Radmacher said that the verb, "usurp authority over," occurs over three hundred times outside the Bible, but only once here in the Word. It is translated by such terms as murder, master, domineer, hold absolute sway over. The word was almost always used with a bad connotation, though its meaning gradually took on changes during the first century. After hours of study, Radmacher asserted, "I do not know at this point what this word means." Then he added that he would be "extremely remiss if [he] were to build a large doctrinal position that affects many people on the basis of what [he] ha[s] to candidly confess before God [he's] not sure."

A recent book presents an erudite case for the possibility that Paul's prohibition against women teachers may have been directed against a specific Gnostic heresy current at Ephesus. This heresy taught that Eve created Adam, and thus was superior to, prior to and the source of Adam. Greek scholar Catherine Kroeger offers an alternative translation of 1 Timothy 2:12-13: "I do not permit woman to teach nor to represent herself as originator of man.... For Adam was created first, then Eve" (Richard Kroeger and Catherine Kroeger, *I Suffer Not a Woman*, Grand Rapids: Baker Books, 1992, p. 103).

If Kroeger's thesis is correrct, it's logical for Paul to speak of the creation order in verse 13, Adam before Eve. On the other hand, others suggest that the creation order is mentioned to lead into the temptation account in verse 14: *Adam was not deceived, but the woman being deceived was in the transgression.* Adam, created first, received firsthand from God the prohibition against eating the fruit, whereas Eve was indirectly informed. Adam sinned with full knowledge, but Eve was deceived. So these verses become a plea for teachers who are trained and mature. The women at Ephesus to which Paul referred, like Eve, were untaught and easily deceived and were leading others astray too. Yet, if instructed, they could be saved while still carrying out their childbearing function. Paul wanted women of all generations to *continue in faith and charity and holiness with sobriety* (vs. 16). And when taught, they could then become teachers themselves, combining motherhood and service in the church.

These verses do not affirm that women as a category are deceived more easily than men. If that were so, says Radmacher, "We should stop letting women teach other women, who are more easily deceived. And we should have women teach men, who are not so easily deceived, and let the men straighten the women out."

Sometimes the charge is made that most heresies stem from women teachers, all the way from Jezebel to Mary Baker Eddy. But church history lists many more serious heresies that have sprung from men. How great our loss if all the doctrinally rich hymns and gospel songs written by women were eliminated from our hymnals. What if all the Sunday school quarterlies and Bible study guides penned by women were to disappear? What about books authored by women, even those which teach authoritatively that women should not teach? Is teaching Scriptural truth via the pen somehow permissible while teaching via the pulpit is a taboo? And what about the extensive contributions of women chairing Christian Education committees?

Summing up my thoughts on these verses that are so frequently cited to silence women's leadership in the church, since scholars disagree so markedly on their meaning, it seems unwise to me to proclaim these puzzling passages as dogmatic doctrinal yardsticks for male-female roles in the church.

EPHESIANS 5:21-28

This passage says that wives should be in submission to their husbands. In later verses, children are told to obey their parents (Ephesians 6:1), and slaves to obey their master (Ephesians 6:5). However, the verb, "to obey with voluntary acquiescence," used of children and slaves, is not used in the relationship of wives to husbands. The verb in Ephesians 5:22, about wives submitting to their husbands, is in the middle voice and means that a wife should take her proper place under her husband, or as some scholars suggest, "identify with her husband," not knuckling under, but expressing unity by becoming one with (Gretchen Gabelein Hull, *Equal To Serve*, Grand Rapids: F.H. Revell Co., 1987, p. 195). When the verb is used in the active voice, it means to subject someone;

it's never used in reference to a husband's conduct towards his wife. A husband is never told to boss or overpower his wife, or "put her where she belongs." Nor is a wife to blindly obey her husband.

Rather, the verse which introduces the section on the duties of wives and husbands, Ephesians 5:21, teaches mutual submission — not just submission of wife to husband, but also of husband to wife. It says, *Submitting yourselves one to another in the fear of the Lord.* It could be translated, "Give way to one another out of reverence for Christ." After speaking to both mates about submission, Paul then addresses the wives, *Be subject to your husbands*, and spends three verses commenting on wifely duty. Next he turns to the husbands, enjoining on them the duty of loving their wives. He thus sets up submission as a two-way street, and, by taking nearly double the verses to elaborate on the husband's duty, seems to give the husband the more difficult assignment.

Both the submission of the wife and the love of the husband are different expressions of the two-dimensional, mutual subjection called for in verse 21. In mutual submission, the sacrificial self-giving of the husband corresponds to the submission and respect required of the wife. C.S. Lewis, who nursed his wife through the ordeal of her illness, says in his book, *The Four Loves*, that headship in marriage means that the husband is to love his wife as Christ loved the church and gave His life for her. He suggests that this headship is most clearly demonstrated in a husband's untiring care and enhancement

for a sick and suffering wife, or in his boundless forgiveness of a bad wife. Christ is upheld as a model,
not of power domination, but of humility, sacrifice,
self-abnegation and forgiveness. Servanthood, not
status, is pre-eminent in male headship that emu-
lates the headship of Christ.

I was to learn later that Dr. John Stott, prominent
Bible teacher and Christian thinker, says that "masculine 'headship' refers to responsibility, rather than
authority" (*Christianity Today*, January 8, 1996, p. 32).

Marriage should be a partnership. Both are leaders. Both are followers. At times a wife gives in to
her husband; on other occasions a husband surren-
ders. They are to *be subject one to another.* Each is
to respond to the needs of the other out of reverence
for Christ. The verb "to have authority over" is
applied to both husband and wife by Paul in his
marital instructions to the Christians. *The wife hath
not power of her own body, but the husband: and
likewise also the husband hath not power of his own
body, but the wife* (1 Corinthians 7:4). This authority is mutual, involving a process of give and take.
One pastor suggested that a successful marriage
requires five bears: bear and 'four'-bear.

Grace Hull, daughter of Dr. Frank Gabelein,
founding headmaster of the Stony Brook School,
said of her parents, "They practiced mutual submission in marriage by each one considering the needs
of the other greater than his or her own. My father
was well-known, but he considered my mother, herself highly educated, as his partner in marriage and

ministry. He always checked his sermons, lectures and articles with my mother for her critical judgment. They planned and discussed school matters and prayed about them together. They were a team, and they laid the foundation of the Stony Brook School as a team. They were the embodiment of the biblical principle that in marriage the two shall become one" (*Equal To Serve*, Grand Rapids: F.H. Revell, 1987, p.34). She never heard her father "put his foot down" in relation to her mother. Unaware of the hierarchical "chain of command" with its rigid male-female roles, she would have been shocked to hear that one was ordained to be "over" the other.

This partner relationship rubbed off on Hull's married life. She said, "If Phil and I heard someone refer to the husband as 'head,' we did not pay much attention, because in our actual practice we saw no need for a 'head' who had final say. Of course at times I got carried away with some project, and Phil had to say, 'No, that's not going to work.' But there were also times when he wanted to do something, and I said, 'No, that's not appropriate.' Neither of us, in putting on the brakes, did so to try to exercise some sort of authority over the other, but because the project did not reflect the best interests of our marital or our family unit. Like all husbands and wives who love and respect each other we did not want to make decisions unilaterally. Although we did not 'bat a thousand' (because nobody's perfect!), we did try to put the interests and the welfare of the other above our own" (pp. 191-192).

Sarah, presented in the New Testament as a model of wifely obedience (1 Peter 3:6), more than once gave orders to her husband, Abraham, who obeyed her (Genesis 16:2; 21:9-10). The ideal woman in Proverbs 31 was her husband's trusted partner, having major responsibility that reached far beyond domestic duties to the management of lands and business in the marketplace. The Talmud has this good advice, "No matter how short your wife is, lean down and take her advice,"

The most serious disagreement between Catherine and William Booth before their marriage concerned women's equality. He felt that a man had more in his head, while a woman had more in her heart. She strongly disagreed, holding that only because of inadequate education did women seem inferior intellectually; by nature they were the equal of men. She said that she would never marry a man who would not give women their proper respect. "She won the argument," comments William Petersen "but a decade later it was her husband who prodded her into preaching, and a decade after that, she was in more demand as a preacher than he was" (Husbands and Wives, Wheaton: Tyndale House Publishers, 1983, p. 63).

It is possible for a wife to hold to male headship in the home and find in a husband's love the freedom and encouragement to unlimited service in the church. Jill Briscoe, popular Bible teacher, said, "It's required, as a wife, to be in proper submission to my husband, and I don't see that in conflict with his responsibility to nurture and cherish me. He will help me find the gifts that God has given me and will insist that I exercise those gifts. If one of those gifts is leadership, my husband, as head of our home, will encourage me to use that gift. So though I believe in male headship in marriage, I don't think this biblical concept is limiting to women in any way" (*Christianity Today*, "Women in Leadership: Finding Ways To Serve The Church," October 3, 1986).

Those who tout male supremacy in marriage quote Ephesians 5:23, *For the husband is the head of the wife, even as Christ is the head of the church.* Scholarship has discovered that the word "head" had a variety of meanings in the ancient world, of which the two most selected by Bible scholars are "authority over" and "source." Catherine Kroeger, a Ph.D. in the area of classical studies, concludes that in the New Testament era this word "rarely had the sense of boss or chief as it does in English and Hebrew." Her paper on the subject, *The Classical Concept of Head as "Source,"* appears in Appendix III in Gretchen Gabelein Hull's book. In Kroeger's view, the husband could be the head of the wife because woman was taken from man's flesh; thus, he is her source. Similarly, Christ as the head of the church is the source from which the church derives its life. Incidentally, a major error of the Eve cult in Ephesus was its claim that woman was the source of man.

HOW INERRANTISTS COULD BE DIVIDED
ON WOMEN PREACHERS

I ended Chapter 5 with a problem. Many fundamentalist pastors around the turn of this century
approved of women preachers and welcomed them to
their pulpits. Many Bible institutes trained women to
be preachers, pastors and Bible teachers. But early
in the century, between World Wars I and II, fundamentalists began to bar women from their pulpits.
Why this change? If early fundamentalists approved
of women's public ministry, why did later fundamentalists oppose this practice? Obviously, one's
belief in biblical inerrancy was not the decisive
answer. Those who held to biblical inspiration stood
on both sides of the question.

I suspect that interpretation, not inspiration, was
a major factor. Admittedly, other reasons con-
tributed, like the opposition of the fundamentalist
movement to the liberation of women during the
World War I period, expressed in their dress, hair
styles, cosmetics, habits of public smoking and
drinking, and entrance into the work force. This
aroused many church leaders who stressed women's
place as in the home in order to buttress family values. Entrance into the pulpit was considered part of
the femininity that could destroy family life.

One of the chief instruments providing ammuni-
tion against the perceived dangers of feminism was a
revised biblical interpretation. Fundamentalists no
longer exegeted 1 Corinthians 14:34 and 1 Timothy

2:11-12 as localized advice for a specific situation. Instead they declared these passages universal commands, revised their earlier stand on women, dug in rigidly with their literalism and thundered loud and frequently, "Let your women keep silence in the churches." Naturally, women who didn't want to disobey the Bible hesitated at following such a calling. Churches, who did not want to be known as denying biblical inerrancy, designated their pulpits, "For Men Only." The early fundamentalists stood on a platform of about half a dozen major doctrinal planks; later fundamentalists added other planks to the platform, among them the silence of women in the churches. Literature upholding women's right to preach dried up. Some groups even labeled women's leadership as a sign of the end time. Such exegesis sealed lips which God might have gifted to speak.

I saw that the person who holds a high view of the Bible must beware of the subtle danger of transferring the inerrancy from the Scriptures to his own interpretation of the Scriptures, thus replacing the authority of Scripture with his own, and setting himself up as the infallible elucidator of the Word. What is authoritative is the Bible — not our explanation of the Bible. On matters not clearly spelled out, such as the issue of women's role in ministry, we must be tolerant of those who come to different conclusions than us, and not brand them as heretics if they are committed to the authority of Scripture. Instead of polarizing our positions, we should continue to present our varying viewpoints with logic and love in the unity of the Spirit.

Reared in the fundamentalist tradition, I had been taught the biblical impropriety of women in the pulpit. Now I saw that perhaps the Scriptural basis for this prohibition wasn't as firm as I had been led to believe. Perhaps I could be loyal to my daughter without being disloyal to the Word. But more pondering was necessary before reaching the end of my journey and coming to my decision.

8

Coming To A Decision

★ ★ ★

In her final year of seminary, Janna submitted
her profile to both national denominational headquarters in Cleveland, Ohio, and to her area minister representative in New York State. The purpose
was to line her up with job openings — churches
looking for a pastor or staff member. Anticipating
graduation in May, 1991, she could look back on an
academic record that would commend her to any
search committee. She was consistently on the
honor roll, and pulled down an "A" in homiletics.
With a 3.79 grade point average in her second year,
she was one of the top two in her class.

But her geographical area of job potential was
considerably limited, since she and her husband had
jointly decided that his work took priority. With a
recent doctoral degree, many years as Director of

Career Development at Hamilton College and Janna's full agreement, Gene had resolved not to seek employment in another part of the country, but rather to pursue the many projects already evolving in his current position. He had invitations to hold seminars, to teach courses at Syracuse University as an adjunct professor and he was writing a book. This meant that Janna's pastoral service had to be confined to a region not too far from home. As she put it to me, "His career comes first."

Not only would job openings be curtailed by distance, but also her type of service. With a pool of fewer available churches, she might not receive a call to pastor a church, nor have frequent opportunities to preach. Perhaps she would seek a ministry in a supporting role: visitation pastor, hospital chaplain or minister of education. When at retirement I gave Janna first choice of the books I did not have room to keep, I noticed that her selection tended more towards the pastoral and leadership titles than to the theological. Perhaps she was more interested in counselling or administrative ministries. Whichever avenue opened up, she knew Gene would be supportive. He often joked about the times he was introduced as the pastor's wife.

As Janna would soon have to make a decision about the type of pastoral ministry she would accept, I knew that I too needed to make up my mind as to the role of women in the church. I had to look at a few more considerations and pick up a few loose threads as I came to the resolution of my problem.

CONSISTENCY OF SCRIPTURE

First Corinthians contains what seems like a contradiction on the role of women in ministry. In Chapter 11, Paul speaks acceptingly of women praying and prophesying in the church service. Not long after, in Chapter 14, he commands women to keep silent in the church. Is there any principle of biblical interpretation to help resolve this and other seeming contradictions in the Scriptures?

A basic rule of hermeneutics says that to understand any individual verse, we must be guided by the complete teaching of all the Scriptural data on that topic. Since the inspiration of the Holy Spirit guarantees the consistency of the Bible so that it cannot contradict itself, we must not only look at each separate passage in its context, but also see how that particular text relates to the entire sweep of teaching on that subject. We must interpret Scripture by Scripture. The whole is the sum of all its parts, each properly integrated.

Failure to grapple with the whole sweep of Scripture can lead to heresy, as in the case of Universalists who hold that all persons will be unconditionally saved. They claim this on the basis of a few detached passages like, *Christ is the Savior of all men*, at the same time neglecting the vast array of Holy Writ which speaks of death and hell, people perishing and lost, going out into eternal darkness. It's dangerous to select isolated verses, yank them from their proper environment, blot out the light thrown on

135

them by other parts of the Bible and then advance them to promote some cherished thesis.

For example, Christian slaveholders in pre-Civil War times defended their practice by quoting Paul's exhortations to slaves to obey their masters, even those oppressing them. But the slaveowners, conveniently or ignorantly, forgot the whole tone of Paul's epistles which teach the attitude of love towards our fellow men and the equality of slave and master in Christ. In time, a correct understanding of the main drive of New Testament teaching brought about the abolition of slavery.

Could there be, I wondered, a disproportionate emphasis on down-grading the role of women in church life when considered against the overwhelming number of approving references in the Bible to women in ministry? In her book, *In Search of God's Ideal Woman*, Dorothy Pope notes that Frederik Franson, a missionary statesman who was influential in the founding of the Evangelical Free Church of America and was the first General Director of The Evangelical Alliance Mission (TEAM), counted every mention in both Old and New Testaments of any kind of speaking ministry or responsible position of women, and came up with nearly one hundred such references (Downers Grove: InterVarsity, 1976, p. 233).

This is a remarkable number considering that there are but two or three references which seem to oppose women's speaking ministry and leadership. Yet these two or three verses have become the rallying point for stifling women. Proper interpretation of the "silencing" verses would seem to call for their integration into the whole teaching of Holy Writ. In other words, 1 Corinthians 14:34 (on silencing) must be comprehended in the light of 1 Corinthians 11 (women praying and prophesying in the church). Universalizing the prohibition of speaking (1 Corinthians 14:34 and 1 Timothy 2:11-12) would propel these passages beyond their purposed scope, as well as produce conflict with other Scriptures. These passages cannot be construed into a denial of the right of women to pray and prophesy under the leading of the Holy Spirit in the church, a right which Paul has already approved.

Integrity demands that we search for the whole counsel of God, which in this case seems to be that, in general, as a rule, women may prophesy in the church service but with certain limitations. A specific kind of speaking is forbidden; women are not to interrupt the assembly, because God does not author confusion. Paul's injunction to women to keep silent in the churches is to be interpreted by the larger law of gospel equality and privilege as expressed in Colossians 3:11. The privilege of female speaking was endorsed and honored, but regulated. No contradiction exists. Paul was no theological schizophrenic. Scripture is consistent.

In an interview in *Christianity Today*, Professor F.F. Bruce, when asked about the role of women, answered, "Paul's teaching in so far as religious status and function are concerned, is that there is no difference between men and women. Anything in Paul's writings that might seem to run contrary to this must be viewed in the light of the main thrust of his teaching and should be looked at with critical scrutiny" (April 7, 1989, p. 24).

Bruce believed that, in interpreting difficult Pauline passages, the one which runs along the line of liberty is much more likely to be true to Paul's intention than one which smacks of bondage or legalism (Kristine Christlieb, "Women and the Collar" in a book review of *Women in Ministry: Four Views, Christianity Today,* April 23, 1990, p. 57).

Another law of biblical interpretation says that a plain Scripture should not be set aside because of another not so easily understood one. In 1 Corinthians 11:4, Paul writes approvingly of women taking part in the church service. But 1 Corinthians 14:34, regarding the silencing of women, is not so clear. The earlier reference should take precedence.

I recalled Dr. Radmacher's statement, quoted in the previous chapter, of his problem with the meaning of the word "authority" in 1 Timothy 2:12, where women are told not to have authority over men. After hours of study he admitted, "I do not know at this point what this word means. I would be extremely remiss if I were to build a large doctrinal position that affects many people on the basis of what I have to candidly confess before God I'm not sure."

WHY ALL MALE APOSTLES?

In some denominations women are excluded from the pastorate because no women were present at the Last Supper, and thus should not be permitted to officiate at it. We could ask, if no women were present at all, then why permit women to even partake of it?

An even more knotty question asks why Jesus never chose a woman among the Twelve. I had wondered the same thing. If Jesus cut across the convention of His day in allowing feminine participation in His ministry, why did He not break that same taboo by choosing women apostles? If He intended women to be pastors, showing their eligibility for equal opportunity in the ministry, why did He not select at least one woman for the Twelve?

Further, when, in the upper room, the one hundred and twenty chose a successor for Judas, why was not one of the women present selected? Likely some women there met the qualifications outlined by Peter. The choice of a woman to the Twelve in either case would have graphically declared the Lord's position on the role of women in His church.

In answer, we turn the question around and ask what would have happened if Jesus had appointed a woman apostle? Simply, it would have been impractical and hazardous for a woman to travel alone as an itinerant missionary in the first-century world. Also, she would not have been accepted as a teacher in many cultures. Many women in religious cult leadership portrayed the image of frenzied emotion.

The fact that in many countries women were not accepted as witnesses may be why Paul did not list any feminine names among the witnesses to the resurrection in his account to the Corinthians (1 Corinthians 15:1-9). Understandably, Jesus chose only male apostles to proclaim the gospel to the first-century era because it was a man's world.

When someone once remarked that all pastors should be male because Jesus chose only males to be His apostles, I asked, "Since all the Twelve were Jews, does that mean that all pastors should be Jews?" We should no more infer from an all-masculine apostleship that the ministry must remain masculine forever, than we should infer from an all-Jewish apostleship that the ministry must remain Jewish forever. Just as Gentile ministers emerged in church history, so the New Testament points beyond the boundary of an all-masculine apostolate. Paul took Greek companions as partners in the ministry; he also thanked God for women fellow-laborers in the gospel.

Knowing that a break with tradition was possible only by degrees, Jesus initiated the process of liberating women from their low status to their place of full equality. In the Gospels, He ascribed them dignity. Women are pictured as the first to see the risen Christ, thus the earliest in the long, distinguished line of women who have boldly borne witness to the victorious Lord. Again the parallel — just as Paul didn't come out clearly to denounce slavery, but set in motion the truths that would ultimately do so, so Jesus, though not appointing any female apostle, certainly launched a course that pointed to the elevation of woman to a place of honorable service in the church.

ARE ELDERS ALWAYS MEN IN THE NEW TESTAMENT?

Those supporting an exclusively male pastorate usually point to 1 Timothy 3:1-2, *If a man desire the office of a bishop, he desireth a good work. A bishop then must be blameless, the husband of one wife.* It should be noted that the word "man" does not occur in the original text, which more accurately reads, *If any one desire....* But it would seem to indicate that bishops (or elders) would be men, and if married, totally devoted to their wives. Similarly, deacons were to "be the husbands of one wife" (1 Timothy 3:12). Again, these officers seem to be men, likewise faithful in a monogamous relationship.

It is true that no woman anywhere in the New Testament is described as being either a bishop or an elder. However, it is equally true that no man is ever described as being a bishop, and the only men specifically cited as elders are Peter (1 Peter 5:1) and the writer of second and third John (verse 1 of each epistle). But several passages mentioning churches that met in homes in those early days (Acts 12:12; 16:40; Romans 16:3-5; 1 Corinthians 1:11; 16:19; Colossians 4:5; Philemon 1), refer to women among the leaders, so we cannot absolutely assume these positions were never held by women. In fact, Paul termed Phoebe a deacon (minister, servant) of the church at Cenchrea (Romans 16:1).

After giving the qualifications of a deacon, Paul then says, *Even so must their wives be grave, not slanderers, sober, faithful in all things* (1 Timothy 3:11). Those who believe that deacons should be men hold that the word "wives" here refers to the wives of deacons, emphasizing the importance of a deacon having a wife of exemplary conduct, befitting his position.

But some believe that the reference is to women deacons. The brevity of the one-verse text makes a firm decision difficult, but some arguments favor the possibility that these are women deacons. For example, no wives are mentioned with the more strategic office of bishop (elder), so why should the wives of deacons be mentioned. Then, the word "women" appears in a context of qualifications about ministers. Could this be the office mentioned in connection with Phoebe? The word "wives" in this verse means "women" in general, whether married or unmarried, depending on the context. Some translators, unconvinced that Paul has the wives of deacons in mind, render the word "women."

From a letter dating back to early secular history comes some support for the existence of women deacons. Pliny the Younger (A.D. 62-113), governor of the Asia Minor province of Bithynia, wrote the Roman Emperor Trajan for counsel regarding the persecution of Christians. Part of his letter reads, "I thought it the more necessary to inquire into the real truth of the matter by subjecting to torture two female slaves who were called 'deacons,' but I found nothing more than a perverse superstition which went beyond all bounds. Therefore, I deferred further inquiry in order to apply to you for a ruling...."

L.E. Maxwell asks, "Did not Pliny choose these two 'female slaves' to torture because they, like Phoebe, held some official position as deacons and could reveal what Christanity was all about?" He concludes, "So we have clear evidence within and without Scripture for the existence of women deacons, or ministers, from early times (L.E. Maxwell with Ruth C. Dearing, *Women in Ministry*, Wheaton: Victor Books, 1987, pp. 68-69).

When Paul urges the choice of a married-to-one-woman elder, the significant factor is not that he is a man, or married, but that he is monogamous. It's the description of a quality that is more important than that he should be a man. Paul is not dealing with gender, but godliness. He would expect the same characteristic in any woman leader — that she be a one-man woman.

In the male-dominated first-century culture, naturally elders would usually be married men. But the Lord Jesus and His apostles, by precept and pattern, propelled the church toward the participation of women in ministry — and possibly feminine leadership. When Paul gave qualifications for elders, he never restricted it to men. No unequivocal command exists barring women from eldership.

ORDINATION OF WOMEN ALREADY WIDELY PRACTICED

Very early in my research I had been surprised to learn of the longstanding and widespread practice of female ordination in many groups within the evangelical sector. Reared in the tradition of post-1930 fundamentalism (I still hold to the basic fundamentals: inspiration of the Bible, virgin birth, substitutionary death, bodily resurrection and second coming of Christ), I was cautioned against women preachers. I was unaware then that many fundamentalists around the turn of the century approved of women preachers, and that the ordination of women had already been practiced for some time.

I also labored under the impression that mainline denominations were the major promoters of female leadership, so I was astonished to read in a *Christianity Today* article that conservative "Denominations in the National Association of Evangelicals have by and large ordained women earlier, in larger numbers, and more consistently than those in the National Council of Churches (Donald W. & Lucille Sider Dayton, "Women as Preachers: Evangelical Precedents," May 23, 1975, p. 4). "One count lists more than 80 Protestant denominations in America that allow the ordination of women" (Roberta Hestenes, "Women in Leadership," *Christianity Today*, October 3, 1986, pp. 6-8).

I discovered that for over a century the Salvation Army has been ordaining women. Many of the

144

evangelical churches founded in the late nineteenth and early twentieth centuries practiced the ordination of women. Founded in 1881, the Church of God (Anderson, Indiana) had as many as 20-25% women among its early preachers and leaders. The Church of the Nazarene, founded in 1894, guaranteed in its original constitution the right of women to preach. As many as one-fifth of its early ministers were women. The Assemblies of God Church has ordained women since its founding in 1914 with women at one time making up to as many as 14% of its ministers. In 1990, delegates to the annual assembly of the more than two million Churches of God (Cleveland, Tennessee) voted to give women authority to perform pastoral duties.

Today the issue is under debate in many evangelical denominations. It seems to me that inevitably the ordination of women will be officially approved by more and more Bible-believing groups until it is generally embraced as common practice. And more and more women will hold the position of senior pastors. J.I. Packer closes his article in *Christianity Today*, titled, "Let's Stop Making Women Presbyters," in a light vein, asking, "Is my cause already lost? Am I crying for the moon? I wait to see, as Oxford men habitually do" (February 11, 1991).

The trend now gaining momentum may well usher in the fulfillment of Catherine Booth's prediction of a century ago, "When the true light shines and God's words take the place of man's traditions, the doctor of divinity who shall teach that Paul commands woman to be silent when God's Spirit urges her to speak, will be regarded much the same as we should regard an astronomer who should teach that the sun is the earth's satellite" (op. cit., p. 13).

DECISION TIME

Here was my problem. Eight years ago I learned that my daughter had experienced an irresistible call to the ministry. Raised in a climate that disapproved of women ministers, I was forced to ask myself how I, myself a pastor, felt about the possibility of having a daughter in the ministry. This book has been the story of my mental and spiritual journey, and I am ready to report my answer. Doubtless I have tipped my hand as to the direction my search has been leading me, so no one will be surprised at the outcome.

Perhaps my conclusion can be stated best in the words of Kenneth S. Kantzer who, wrapping up a series of articles in *Christianity Today* on women in leadership, both pro and con, wrote, "What shall we do about the increasing number of highly gifted and well-trained women seeking to use their gifts and to minister in the church? The answer would seem to be very simple: If Scripture does not forbid, ordain them and encourage them to teach in the church."

Kantzer said that we dare not "ignore the immense potential of the divinely given skills that many women possess to teach and lead the church. On the contrary, we must encourage them in their exercise of those gifts.... The church suffers from a dearth of solid, scripturally sound teaching and from a dangerous void of leadership. Women could supply more and more of these crucial services were we more open to their ministry. Our failure to utilize their skills becomes more and more irrational in the light of the role of women in the society around us." He added that the church "loses also because increasingly it is turning our finest women away from a church that they see not as the body of Christ where we are all one in the Lord, but as a male pre-serve that selfishly seeks to cling to worldly power in the name of Christ. Like the ancient Pharisees, we twist the Scripture to suit our own ends."

These are strong words, but Kantzer softened them by advising us to proceed with care. For the sake of the "weaker" brother, or out of respect for cultural customs, "it is seldom wise or expedient to run roughshod over another's values or beliefs, espe-cially in areas of biblical interpretation. In order not to offend others who are convinced (mistakenly, we believe) that the Bible forbids women to teach, in certain situations we must choose not to ordain women for the sake of the gospel."

But Kantzer did not back off on his support of women's ordination. He said, "This does not mean we set aside our concern for the status of women in the church. If anything, we must intensify our efforts to bring others to a proper understanding of Scrip-ture. But we do this with grace and sensitivity. We must consistently teach what the Scriptures really say on this important point. Further, it is the special

responsibility of men to make the church aware of
this teaching and to give solid support to women who
possess gifts of teaching and leadership (Copyright-
ed by *Christianity Today*, October 3, 1986, pp. 15-
18, and used by permission).

Thoughts on Ordination

Ordination means different things to different
people. In some denominations, ordination means
entrance to an office which gives authority in the
church to teach and to baptize and to preside at the
Lord's table. To the government, ordination gives the
right to marry, qualify for the military chaplaincy
and receive certain tax benefits, like not having to
include housing allowance as income on IRS 1040.
And to others, the laying on of hands at the climax
of an ordination service carries no sacred unction,
but rather signifies human acknowledgment of a
previous divine anointing. To them, this symbolic
gesture, rich and beautiful, says in effect, "We con-
firm that God has laid His hand on you. We recog-
nize your divine call. As fellow servants we join with
you in unity. As you go, we go with you."

To others, ordination is extra-biblical and should
not be practiced. One of the early Plymouth Brethren
leaders, John Nelson Darby, argued that if the Holy
Spirit has bestowed spiritual gifts on all believers,
then for a clergyman to arrogate to himself the sole
right to preside at communion and direct the entire
service is to deny the work of the Holy Spirit. He

used strong words in titling his booklet, *The Notion of a Clergyman: The Sin against the Holy Ghost in This Generation.* The noted Baptist preacher, Charles Haddon Spurgeon, refused to submit to the ceremony because of the exaggerated importance placed on it by the liturgical churches. He called it "idle hands laid on empty heads."

Biblical basis for ordination, as we know it today, is skimpy. Our ordination procedures are not built on specific exegesis of Scriptural passages. The Gospels do not record that Jesus laid hands on the apostles, either when He called them or when He gave them the Great Commission, though He did breathe on them the Holy Spirit.

Twice in Acts the laying on of hands appears to have conveyed the gift of the Holy Spirit (Acts 8:17; 19:6). The laying on of hands of the seven deacons was for a specific work of serving others (Acts 6:6). Ananias laid hands on the newly converted Paul that he might receive his sight and be filled with the Spirit (Acts 9:17). Barnabas and Paul were commissioned with the laying on of hands for a particular mission to the Gentiles (Acts 13:1-3), which they fulfilled (Acts 14:3). This was not like ordination today, for Paul and Barnabas were already in the ministry, and on this occasion were "ordained" for a definite mission.

When Paul and Barnabas "ordained" elders in fledgling churches on their first missionary journey (Acts 14:23), the word means "appointed"; nothing is said of laying on of hands. It is not necessary to assume that the laying on of hands in 1 Timothy 4:14 and 2 Timothy 1:16 is an example of ordination. Rather, a spiritual gift was imparted or confirmed to Timothy; it was not his installation into some office or post of authority. The laying on of hands in the New Testament cannot be identified with any uniform rite practiced in the early church. In reality, no New Testament passage deals with ordination to ceremonial office as we conceive of the ceremony today.

The laying on of hands in the New Testament church seems more to do with service than rank or authority. This fits the New Testament concept of leadership which is always seen more in terms of service than status. Jesus repeatedly told His throne-aspiring disciples that the one who wants to be chief should be servant. Elders were not to "lord it over the flock" (1 Peter 5:3). Interestingly, one title commonly given church leaders is "minister," simply another word for "servant." Because the New Testament church did not ordain people to stations of authority, but appointed them to avenues of service, many see no difficulty in ordaining women as pastors today. Others would ordain women as ministers of children, of education, of visitation, but would reserve the eldership, or senior pastor position, to a male. But then comes the question, "If willing to ordain women to every other spot of ministry on a church staff, why refrain from taking that last step of ordaining women as senior pastors?"

Women Needed

Missionary leader Fredrik Franson gave this analogy. He imagined dozens of people tossed overboard from a ship accident, about to drown. A few men immediately try to save them, and everyone applauds. But look yonder, a few women have untied a boat to join in the rescue. Immediately some men, standing idly by, with plenty of time on their hands, cry out, "No, no, women must not help; rather let the people drown." Commented Franson, "What stupidity!" (op, cit., *No Time for Silence*, p. 145).

History emphatically records the vital part women have played in rescuing the lost and edifying the saints. Without their ministry, the church would have been severely retarded. Who knows what might have been accomplished had some of God's choicest servants not been sorely criticized and pointlessly stymied. A graduate of Prairie Bible Institute sailed on the Queen Mary in 1960 as a missionary headed for Borneo. At the suggestion of the mission head, before boarding she received permission from the purser to lead the Protestant service in the large lounge area. Although a shy, twenty-nine year-old, first-term missionary, she selected the hymns, planned the order of service and spoke to a hundred people, including thirty returning missionaries. Many came to shake her hand. But one missionary, a male, pressed a tract into her hand and told her to read it back in her stateroom. The thrust of the tract was, "It's a sin for women to preach!" Someone suggested that the male missionary may not have had either the initiative or the courage to witness the way she did.

In the early years of women's work on the foreign field, a missionary to China was recalled by her board because of the complaints that she was overstepping her sphere as a woman, even taking it upon herself to preach. She replied that her field had village after village that was unreached with the gospel, and that she, with a national woman, had gone into the country, gathered groups of men, women and children and told them the story of the cross. "If this is preaching," she said, "I plead guilty to the charge." One of the board members asked, "Have you ever been ordained to preach?" She answered, "No," then with great dignity, "but I believe I have been fore-ordained!"

Gifts Are To Be Exercised

G. Campbell Morgan, in private correspondence, made this strong statement: "There are one or two simple facts which, if borne in mind, ought to settle the question whether women should teach or preach. First, *In Christ there can be no male and female.* Second, fitness for ministry in the Church consists in the possession of a gift bestowed by the Holy Spirit. Third, the Spirit bestows His gifts upon each one severally as He will. If the Holy Spirit bestows upon some woman a gift in the ministry of the Word, no ecclesiastical organization has any right to prevent her exercising that gift, and there certainly ought to be room in our churches for the exercise of every gift bestowed by the Head of the Church through the Spirit, without reference to nationality, social position, or sex, for these things are abolished in Christ" (edited by Jill Morgan, *This Was His Faith: Expository Letters of G. Campbell Morgan*, Grand Rapids: Baker Books, 1977, p. 120).

I had reached my decision. My fidelity to the Scriptures as God's inspired and infallible Word would not be compromised by my loyalty to my daughter Janna, should she become an ordained minister of the gospel. I would most certainly be happy to address her with the proper (though man-made) title, "The Reverend Janna Roche."

Janna graduated from Colgate-Rochester Divinity School on May 4, 1991 with the degree of M.Div. (Master of Divinity). The service included the hymns, "All Hail the Power of Jesus' Name," "Amazing Grace" and "We've Come This Far by Faith." About half of the fifty or so graduates were women. She was among six who graduated with distinction, all women.

Planning Christian ministry in one form or another, she pondered several leads. Starting the first Sunday in July, she became the regular supply preacher in the downtown Utica (New York) United Church of Christ Church as they searched for a new pastor. With a strong interest in the care of the terminally ill, she signed up for a ten-week summer course in Hospice Volunteer training.

During the summer, Janna accepted the invitation to become the acting Protestant Chaplain at Hamilton College in Clinton, New York, for the coming school year. Her full title read, "Coordinator of the Chaplaincy and Protestant Chaplain." She also accepted the position of Pastoral Coordinator of Hospice Care, which involved monitoring the pastoral care of hospice patients in three counties in the Utica area. Both positions were part-time.

She applied for ordination through her denominational channels, passed her ordination examination in late July and was duly ordained on Sunday, August 25 in an impressive and well-attended service in the lovely chapel of Hamilton College. About a dozen clergymen participated. At her invitation I also took part, giving the charge to the new minister. I began by saying, "It's a delight to have a share in the ordination service of my daughter, but I am going to have a difficult time learning to call her 'Reverend.'" I also added that this was not the first time I had given her a charge! My challenge to her, based on Paul's exhortation in 1 Timothy 4:12-16, was to proclaim the Word, pattern the life and persevere to the end.

In our hotel room that evening, turning the pages of the local paper, *The Clinton Courier*, I came to the listing of churches. Included was an announcement which I pointed out to my wife, who from the beginning enthusiastically approved of Janna's decision to enter the ministry. The newspaper item read:

Hamilton College
Hamilton College Chapel, Clinton
Janna Roche, Protestant Chaplain
Church services begin September 1st

Epilogue

★ ★ ★

Janna's chaplaincy job description included responsibility for Protestant worship, visitation of hospitalized professors and students, co-ordination of Jewish and Catholic chaplains, and advising volunteer action ministries, including rescue mission, rape crisis center, AIDS coalition, student tutors, abused wives and homeless shelters.

Her hospice ministry involves overseeing the delivery of pastoral care to hospice patients and families requesting it, and assisting in support groups for staff, families, nurses and social workers.

During her first year, she conducted two weddings at the college and ten funerals, mostly hospice patients. One funeral was that of a nineteen-year-old college student, a victim of leukemia.

During her first year (1991-92), Janna was the

acting chaplain. In August 1992, the college appointed her the first, regular, full-time female chaplain. Hamilton College is a select, liberal arts college with a student body of over sixteen hundred. She continued to devote significant service to hospice, a ministry close to her heart. She averages at least two funerals a month.

As part of her chaplaincy ministry, Janna invites outside speakers from time to time. She brought Keith Miller, author of *The Taste of New Wine* to the campus in 1993.

She arranged for Tony Campolo to speak in November, 1994. The feature editor of the college newspaper, reviewing Campolo's lecture, wrote, "Each member of the audience had felt the heat of Tony Campolo's fire that evening and in many it will continue to burn for days and weeks to come. No person left the Chapel last Thursday unaffected.... Campolo was without doubt one of the most successful speakers that Hamilton has seen in a very long time."

Toward the end, Campolo challenged students to come to Philadelphia in the summer and work without pay to help build homes in the inner city. Dozens flocked to the front to give him their names for more information, and some did go to help the following summer. Janna has sent many students on similar assignments on school breaks, including three groups to Miami to help with Habitat for Humanity.

Janna frequently fills the pulpits of nearby churches. She recently spoke at the chapel at Colgate

University and received an unusual reaction. After the service and the passing of the peace, a student shook her hand. "Could I have a copy of your sermon to hang in our bathroom suite?" she asked.

Taken back by this request, and wondering if she had heard right, Janna replied, "Excuse me?"

The student explained, "That's where we hang all our important reading material!"

On reading the story of my journey and the destination at which I arrived, I suspect that some of you may be saying that I changed my mind because it was my daughter who was involved. But in looking back, I realize that previous to my investigation into the matter I really had no opinion to change. Though raised in an environment of disapproval of women preachers, I had gone along with this view uncritically. So I did not hold any conviction on the issue for I had never given the matter much study. But now I do have a conviction. I am now convinced that a woman may preach, teach men and be ordained as a senior pastor. As I think back on my forty years as pastor of the same church, I recall frequently inviting women speakers into the pulpit in our Sunday morning service, both missionaries and Bible teachers. I also recall permitting women to teach adult classes which included men. And I also remember the objections I invariably received on such occasions.

A telling argument that kept occurring repeatedly throughout all my searching was this: If the Holy Spirit confers upon a woman a gift in the ministry of the Word, who has the right to deny that woman the place in the church that permits her to properly exercise that gift allocated by the Head of the church through the Spirit? And, as a result, are we missing out on the divine provision to help meet the massive need for the ministry of gifted workers? And what about accountability in the day of judgment for forbidding or discouraging some woman from using her gift in the local church?

Missionary statesman Robert E. Speer may have hit the nail on the head when he said, "God shuts no doors to His daughters which He opens to His sons."

At this writing, Janna is now completing her fifth year as chaplain at Hamilton College. Whether she continues in the chaplaincy or accepts a pastorate or devotes full time to hospice, her mother and I pray that our daughter will always use her gifts as a good and faithful servant of Jesus Christ.